WEB DESIGN
SOURCEBOOK

Diseño de páginas web Design de páginas web Design di pagine web

promopress

WEB DESIGN SOURCEBOOK

Diseño de páginas web Design de páginas web Design di pagine web

Cristian Campos

Web Design Sourcebook
Diseño de páginas web Design de páginas web Design di pagine web

Editorial coordination: Cristian Campos
Texts: Cristian Campos, Laura Higes Castillo
Translation: Cillero & de Motta
Art direction: Emma Termes Parera
Layout assistant: Leticia Mazaira

PROMOPRESS is a brand of:
PROMOTORA DE PRENSA INTERNACIONAL, S. A.
Ausiàs March, 124
08013 Barcelona, Spain
Tel.: +34 93 245 14 64
Fax: +34 93 265 48 83
E-mail: info@promopress.es
www.promopress.es
www.promopresseditions.com

First published in English / Spanish / Portuguese / Italian: 2012
ISBN: 978-84-92810-42-0
Printed in China

ler Alınır, Neler Satılır?

Introduction

With nearly 2 billion web pages currently circulating on the net, standing out is a must to create a webpage that appeals to the internet surfer and makes them want to continue to surf the web. The web designer must create an attractive design to attract and retain visitors, focusing on the structure and hierarchy of the website and also the use of color, the typography and the implementation of multimedia applications, among other aspects. The introduction of programmes such as HTML5 and CSS3 has made it easier for novice designers to create a webpage without having advanced programming skills.

This book will reveal the latest tendencies in the field of web design from the sample of the work of dozens of international designers, all who have the same objective: inject their creativity into the functionality of the web, depending on whether it is an informative or corporate website, a social network or the portfolio of an artist, among other formats, opting for a continuously evolving support that is more accessible and offers more possibilities for artistic creation.

Introducción

Con cerca de 2.000 millones de páginas web circulando en la actualidad en la red, se hace necesario diferenciarse con el objetivo de crear una web que llame la atención del internauta para que siga navegando. El diseñador web tiene, así, la función de crear un diseño lo suficientemente atractivo como para atraer y fidelizar a los visitantes ocupándose de la estructura y jerarquización de la página, pero también del uso del color, la elección de la tipografía, o la implementación de aplicaciones multimedia, entre otros aspectos. La implantación de programas como el HTML5 y el CSS3 han facilitado que diseñadores no expertos puedan crear una página web sin tener grandes nociones de programación.

En este libro, el lector conocerá las últimas tendencias en el ámbito del diseño de páginas web, a partir de la muestra del trabajo de decenas de diseñadores internacionales, todos ellos con un objetivo en común: poner su creatividad al servicio de la funcionalidad de la web –en función de si se trata de una web informativa, corporativa, una red social o el portafolio de un artista, entre otros formatos– y apostando por un soporte en constante evolución y que cada vez resulta más accesible y ofrece más posibilidades para la creación artística.

Introdução

Com cerca de dois mil milhões de páginas web a circular actualmente na rede, torna-se necessário diferenciar-se com o objectivo de criar uma página web que chame à atenção do internauta para que continue a navegar. O web designer tem desta forma a função de criar um design suficientemente apelativo que para além de atrair e fidelizar os visitantes ocupando-se da estrutura e hierarquização da página web, também se ocupa da utilização da cor, da escolha da tipografia, e da implementação de aplicações multimédia, entre outros aspectos. A implantação de programas como o HTML5 e o CSS3 permitem que designers não entendidos possam criar uma página web sem ter grandes noções de programação.

Neste livro o leitor conhecerá as últimas tendências no âmbito do design de páginas web, a partir da exposição do trabalho de dezenas de designers internacionais, todos eles com um objectivo em comum: colocar a sua criatividade ao serviço da funcionalidade da web (dependendo de se tratar de uma web informativa, corporativa, uma rede social ou o portefólio de um artista, entre outros formatos) e apostando num suporte em constante evolução e que cada vez se torna mais acessível e oferece mais possibilidades para a criação artística.

Introduzione

Con quasi due miliardi di pagine web attualmente presenti in rete, è necessario differenziarsi per creare una pagina web che richiami l'attenzione dell'internauta affinché questi continui a esplorarla. Il web designer ha dunque la funzione di creare un progetto abbastanza accattivante da attrarre e fidelizzare gli utenti occupandosi della struttura e della gerarchizzazione della pagina web, ma anche dell'uso del colore, della scelta degli elementi tipografici o dell'implementazione di applicazioni multimediali, solo per citare alcuni aspetti. L'affermarsi di programmi come HTML5 e CSS3 ha consentito a programmatori non esperti di creare una pagina web senza avere grandi nozioni di programmazione.

In questo libro il lettore scoprirà le ultime tendenze nel campo del design delle pagine web partendo da un campione del lavoro di decine di designer internazionali, aventi tutti un obiettivo comune: mettere la propria creatività al servizio della funzionalità web – a seconda del tipo di sito, informativo, aziendale, social network o il portfolio di un artista, solo per citare alcuni esempi –, scommettendo su un supporto in costante evoluzione, ogni volta più accessibile e in grado di offrire maggiori possibilità per la creazione artistica.

DEEP TIME

A HISTORY OF THE EARTH – INTERACTIVE INFOGRAPHIC

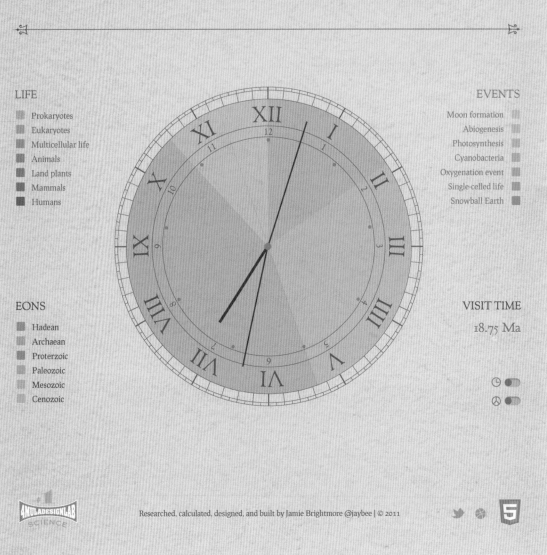

LIFE

- Prokaryotes
- Eukaryotes
- Multicellular life
- Animals
- Land plants
- Mammals
- Humans

EVENTS

- Moon formation
- Abiogenesis
- Photosynthesis
- Cyanobacteria
- Oxygenation event
- Single-celled life
- Snowball Earth

EONS

- Hadean
- Archaean
- Proterzoic
- Paleozoic
- Mesozoic
- Cenozoic

VISIT TIME

18.75 Ma

Researched, calculated, designed, and built by Jamie Brightmore @jaybee | © 2011

★ PRESENTING AN HTML5 INTERACTIVE INFOGRAPHIC ★

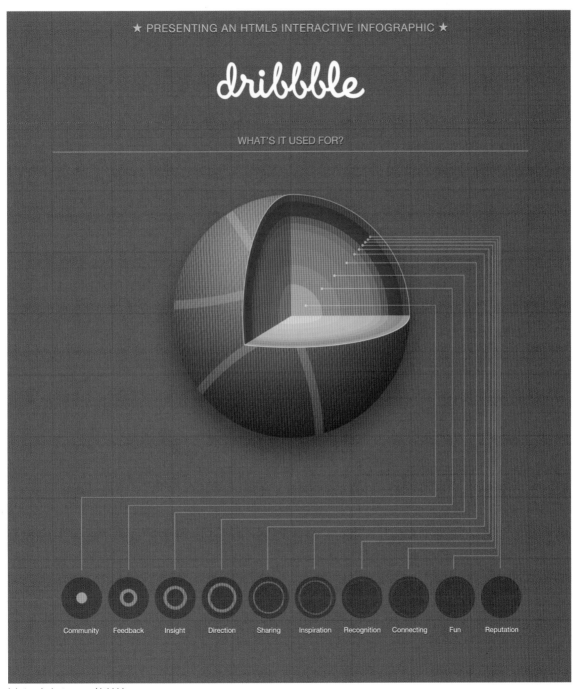

WHAT'S IT USED FOR?

Community   Feedback   Insight   Direction   Sharing   Inspiration   Recognition   Connecting   Fun   Reputation

lab.4muladesign.com/dribbble

galeriavertice.com

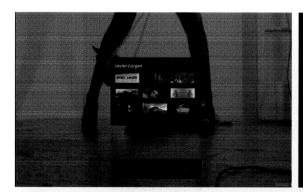

www.javierlargen.com

www.newtownlab.com

arbel-designs.com

www.koziol.de

sharenow.com

www.shoppimon.com

cliqasia.com

www.thewhiterabbit.com.sg

www.98800.org

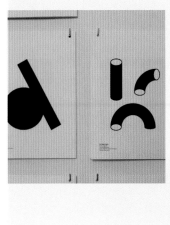

www.98800.org/wemakesigns

Home About Contacts Credits OTA Odin teatret

ODIN TEATRET ARCHIVES

The Document Archives
The Photographic Archives
The Audiovisual Archives
Oral Sources
The Living Archives

THE
ARC
HIV
ES

Home About Contacts Credits OTA Odin teatret

ODIN TEATRET ARCHIVES | Odin streaming | odinteatret.dk

The Archives
Odin Story

Los Archivos
Historia del Odin

The site "Odin Teatret Archives" is not an on-line
archive. It merely shows the contents of Odin
Teatret Archives through a series of examples
which also provide glimpses of Odin Teatret's vi-
sions, history, multifaceted activities and its net
of relationships covering a period of more than
forty five years.

*El sitio web "Archivos del Odin Teatret" no es
un archivo on-line. Nuestra someramente los
contenidos de los archivos del Odin Teatret a
través de una serie de ejemplos que permiten
vislumbrar también las visiones, la historia, las
polifacéticas actividades del Odin Teatret y su
red de relaciones que se extiende por más de
cuarenta y cinco años.*

JERZY GROTOWSKI
TOWARDS
A POOR

Home About Contacts Credits OTA Odin teatret

ODIN TEATRET ARCHIVES | THE ARCHIVES

The Document Archives
   Fonds Eugenio Barba
   Fonds Odin Teatret
   Fonds Iben Nagel Rasmussen
   Fonds Cristina Wistari Formaggia
The Photographic Archives
The Audiovisual Archives
Oral Sources
The Living Archives

The Document Archives (intro)

Consultation of the documents at the Odin Teatret Archives has been
facilitated by a series of "inventories" (published on this site as work in
progress). These inventories describe and contextualise the patrimony of
documents and audio-visuals, as well as the maze of historical situations,
coincidences and contingencies from which they were born.

read more...

www.odinteatretarchives.com

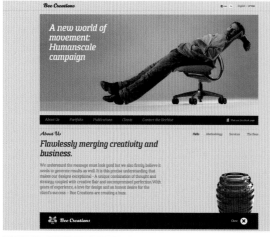

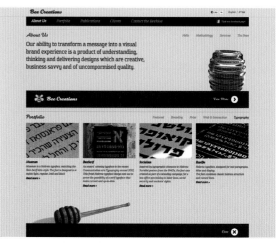

www.bee-creations.com

< 24

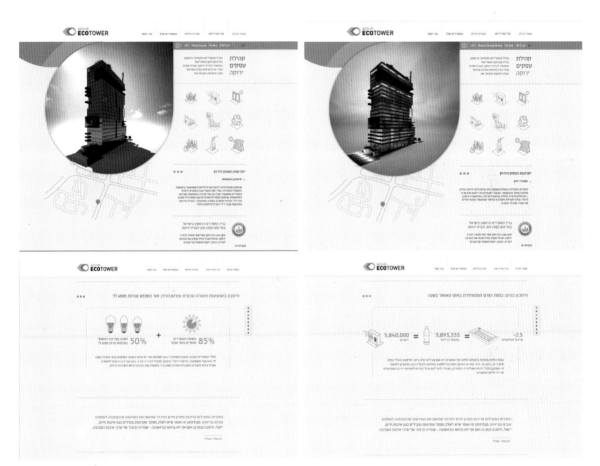

www.ecotower.co.il

BENDERTAINMENT
GRAFIC & WEBDESIGN

BENDERTAINMENT
GRAFIC & WEBDESIGN

NEWS PORTFOLIO WEB PRINT CONTACT CLIENTS ABOUT IMPRINT

Bendertainment Grafic and Webdesign
I am a freelance web and graphic designer based in Berlin,
specialized in building custom web and print design, logo
and apparel design. After working for a popular Streetwear
Label, i started up my own business called Bendertainment
I love taking up challenges and seizing the chance to push
my skills to a higher ground. When i'm not sitting behind
my desk, i'm out for skate or make my six string Les Paul
scream
www.bendertainment.com

www.bendertainment.com

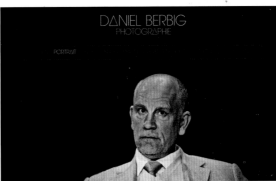

www.berbig-photographie.de

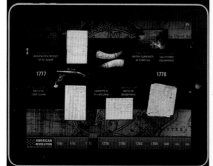

stevemccurry.com

easternstate.org

explorer.muralarts.org

1931

LIBERATION OF THE PEON

In *Liberation of the Peon*, Rivera developed a
harrowing narrative of corporal
punishment. A laborer, beaten and left to
die, is cut down from a post by sympathetic
revolutionary soldiers, who tend to his
broken body. Peonage—a system of
indentured servitude established by
Spanish colonizers, under which natives
were forced to work the land—persisted in
Mexico into the 20th century. The mural

THE MURAL IN-DEPTH

+ CAPTION

1931

INDIAN WARRIOR

Of all the panels Rivera made for The
Museum of Modern Art, *Indian Warrior*
reaches back farthest into Mexican history,
to the Spanish Conquest of the early 16th
century. An Aztec warrior wearing the
costume of a jaguar stabs an armored
conquistador in the throat with a stone
knife. The Spaniard's steel blade—an
emblem of European claims to superiority
—lies broken nearby. Jaguar knights,

THE MURAL IN-DEPTH

MURALS

CHRONOLOGY

RIVERA'S
NEW YORK

MATERIALS &
TECHNIQUE

moma.org/interactives/exhibitions/2011/rivera/intro.php

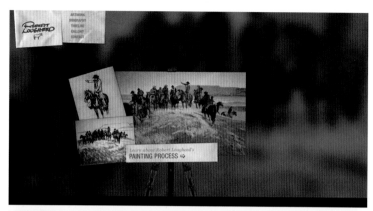

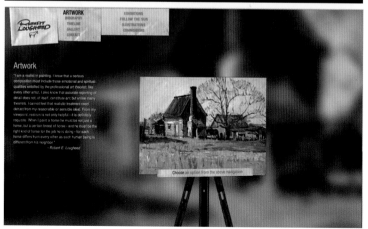

robertlougheed.com

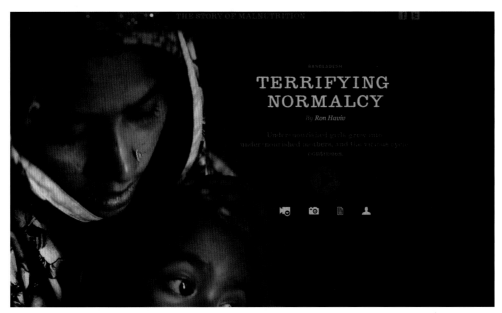

THE STORY OF MALNUTRITION

BANGLADESH

TERRIFYING NORMALCY

By Ron Haviv

Under-nourished girls grow into
under-nourished mothers, and the vicious cycle
continues.

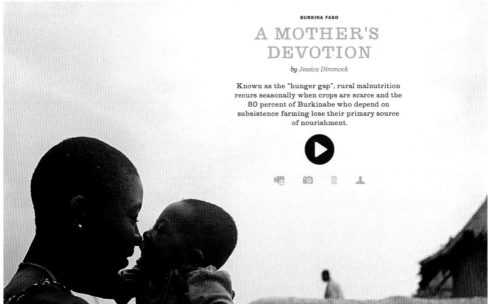

BURKINA FASO

A MOTHER'S DEVOTION

by Jessica Dimmock

Known as the "hunger gap", rural malnutrition
recurs seasonally when crops are scarce and the
80 percent of Burkinabe who depend on
subsistence farming lose their primary source
of nourishment.

starvedforattention.org

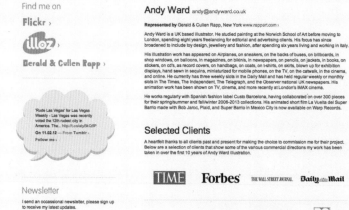

ANDY WARD
Illustration.

Working overtime,
undertime, anytime,
all the time.

HOME PORTFOLIOS BLOG STORE CONTACT/INFO

Find me on

Flickr ›

illoz ›

Gerald & Cullen Rapp ›

'Rude Las Vegas' for Las Vegas
Weekly - Las Vegas was recently
voted the 12th rudest city in
America. The... http://t.co/atyBkQ9P
On 11.02.12 · From Tumblr
Follow me ›

Newsletter

I send an occasional newsletter, please sign up
to receive my latest updates.

Your email address   Go ›

Andy Ward andy@andyward.co.uk

Represented by Gerald & Cullen Rapp, New York www.rappart.com ›

Andy Ward is a UK based illustrator. He studied painting at the Norwich School of Art before moving to
London, spending eight years freelancing for editorial and advertising clients. His focus has since
broadened to include toy design, jewellery and fashion, after spending six years living and working in Italy.

His illustration work has appeared on Airplanes, on sneakers, on the backs of buses, on billboards, in
shop windows, on balloons, in magazines, on bikinis, in newspapers, on pencils, on jackets, in books, on
stickers, on cd's, as record covers, on handbags, on coats, on t-shirts, on skirts, blown up for exhibition
displays, hand sewn in sequins, miniaturized for mobile phones, on the TV, on the catwalk, in the cinema,
and online. He currently has three weekly slots in the Daily Mail and has held regular weekly or monthly
slots in The Times, The Independent, The Telegraph, and the Observer national UK newspapers. His
animation work has been shown on TV, cinema, and more recently at London's IMAX cinema.

He works regularly with Spanish fashion label Custo Barcelona, having collaborated on over 300 pieces
for their spring/summer and fall/winter 2006-2013 collections. His animated short film La Vuelta del Super
Barrio made with Bob Jaroc, Plaid, and Super Barrio in Mexico City is now available on Warp Records.

Selected Clients

A heartfelt thanks to all clients past and present for making the choice to commission me for their project.
Below are a selection of clients that show some of the various commercial directions my work has been
taken in over the first 10 years of Andy Ward illustration.

TIME   Forbes   THE WALL STREET JOURNAL   Daily Mail

theguardian   THE SUNDAY TIMES   Macworld   PC MAGAZINE

ART LOVE WORLD
Create. Raise. Donate.

About Us

Delivery & Returns

Contact Us

What is Art Love World?

Art Love World has been setup to raise money for various charities through design. Products will be available from this site to purchase and each year we will be hosting an event for a chosen charity.

Art Love World Live!

Art Love World will be hosting its first ever live event as part of this year's Norwich Fringe Festival at the Norwich Arts Centre on May 20th. The event is being held in aid of the earthquake and tsunami in Japan, and all profits will go straight to a charity providing relief for Japan.

The event will showcase some of the finest talents from East Anglia, including fantastic live bands, comedians, poets, beatboxer, magician and DJs so you can get your groove on for the evening, in addition to a host of other spectacular treats in store on the night.

Music acts will include the rock, funk and jazz fusion of The Fuzz, the Lou Reed-esque sound of Axel Loughrey, the stunning singer-songwriter Gracie Wright, the talented and soulful Jordan Jackson, the diverse acoustic duo Cielo and, last but not least, the fantastic Norwich Ukulele Society.

Other acts include the hilarious and talented comic poet Tim Clare, the hilariously humble wit of Adam Warne, the acerbic hippie wit of comedian Andy Bennett and Chris Farnell, one of Norwich's finest wits. As well as some surprising walkabout performances

This is one event not to be missed and it's all for a great cause.

Time 7.30-1.00am

Tickets available direct from Norwich Art Centre on 01603 660352

www.artloveworld.com

the band history

The Pineapple Thief was formed by Bruce Soord, in 1999. Initially a solo studio project, the band has grown into a globally gigging outfit, with 7 albums under their belt and an ever increasing army of fans throughout the world. The band name is derived from an obscure American film called Eve's Bayou, in which there is a scene where a young girl steals a pineapple (Scene 29 on the DVD release is titled 'Pineapple Thief').

Previous reviews have drawn comparisons to, among others, Radiohead, Sigur Ros, Pink Floyd, Elbow and Muse but their recent releases – Tightly Unwound (2008) and Someone Here Is Missing (2010) – are testament to a band who have moved beyond these influences to create their own unique sound. Add to this a live show that is currently wowing crowds across Europe and you find The Pineapple Thief barnstorming their way into your musical psyche.

Like most bands, the Thief grew from humble beginnings. Their debut album 'Abducting the Unicorn' rose from the ashes of Bruce's former band, 'Vulgar Unicorn' and was released on the little known underground label Cyclops Records. The idea was to create a vehicle to realise Bruce's personal musical ambitions. Initial sales were slow. However, a glowing review in a major Dutch publication pushed the band through to a waiting and eager fan base.

Encouraged by this, Bruce ventured back into the studio and released the follow up, '137' in 2001. A third album, 'Variations on a Dream' followed two years later. Remarkably for such a small label, sales continued to grow and fans continued to climb on board. It was the increasing demands from fans for a live performance that inevitably led to the formation of a full band which originally consisted of former university mate Jon Sykes

www.pineapplethief.com

www.sickcityclub.net

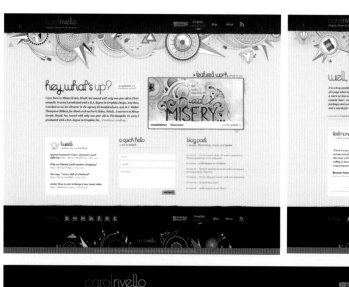

haisushibar.com.br

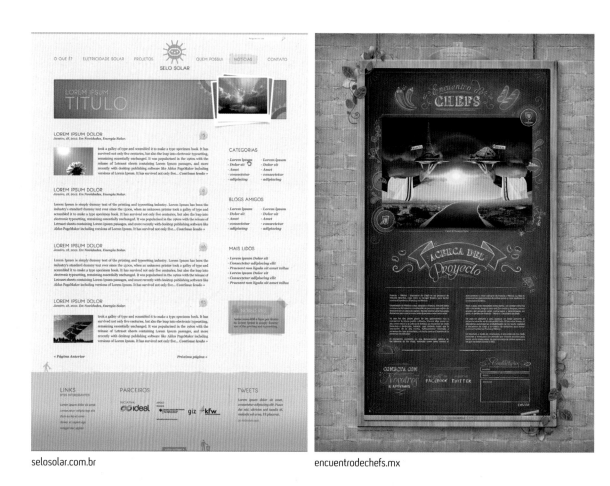

selosolar.com.br

encuentrodechefs.mx

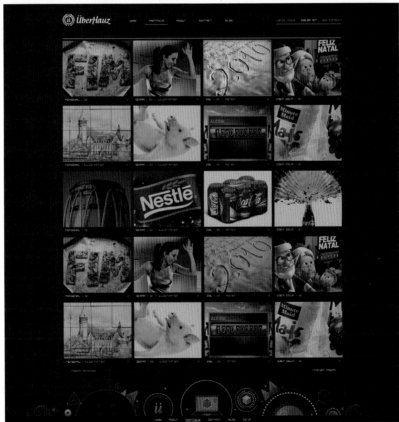

uberhauz.com

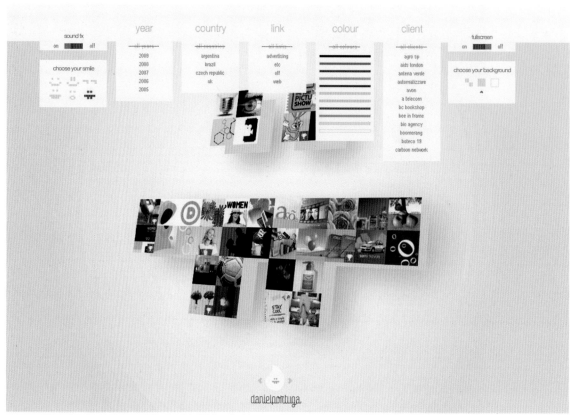

www.danielportuga.com

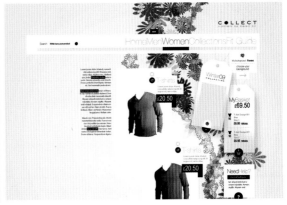

www.automatizzare.com.br

beeinframe.com

www.telefonica.com.br

www.mars.com

www.thebioagency.com

marianavgomes.com

www.edding.com

www.laufen.de

www.nike.com/nikeos/p/nke6/en_EMEA/air_style

www.nike.com/nikeos/p/nke6/en_EMEA/air_style

www.charitea.com

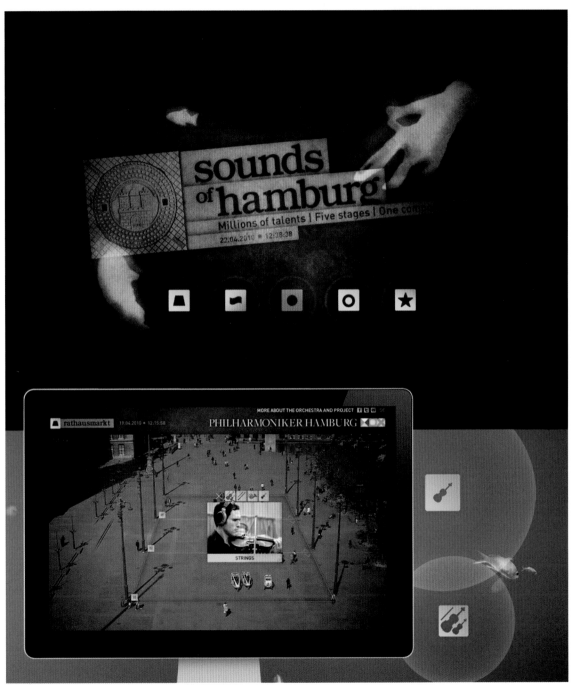

www.philharmoniker-hamburg.de/sounds_of_hamburg/index.html

www.beancounteraz.com

OPEN 7 DAYS A WEEK

CANTILEVER

FISH · CHIPS

LATCHFORD
01925 656590

HOME · MENU · HISTORY · FIND US

Menu

CHIPS	REGULAR £1.30		
	LARGE £1.80		
COD _____ £3.30			
SAUSAGE	SMALL 80p		
	MEDIUM £1.00		
BEANS £1.00	BIGFOOT £1.20		
FRUITY CURRY 4oz 70p 6oz £1.00			
CHINESE CURRY " 70p " £1.00			
GRAVY _____ " 70p " £1.00			
PEAS UNSALTED " 70p " £1.00			

HOLLAND'S PIES

MEAT & POTATO
STEAK & KIDNEY   ALL
MINCED BEEF & ONION
CHEESE & ONION £1.40
CHICKEN & MUSHROOM

MEAT
CORNISH PASTIE
STEAK & KIDNEY PUDDING
PEPPERED STEAK PIE

CHICKEN BREAST	£3.30
CHICKEN NUGGETS (8)	£2.70
CHIP BARM _____	£1.70
CHICKEN BURGER } +BARM	
BEEF BURGER }	£2.20
BATTER EXTRA _____	20p
SCAMPI (10) _____	£3.70
SPAM FRITTER	£1.80
CHOP SUEY ROLL	£1.60
FISH CAKE	90p
BOILED RICE	£1.40
GRATED CHEESE	50p
BARM CAKE _____	50p

CANS 70p   WATER 80p

The Craft Cotton Co.

www.thecraftcottonco.co.uk/   RSS   Q▾ Google

CALL US TODAY: 0161 0832 2213   FIND A FABRIC: Search description

THE CRAFT COTTON Co.

HOME   ABOUT US   OUR FABRIC RANGE   SEE A REPRESENTATIVE   CONTACT US

MY BASKET 1   MY SAMPLES 1

YOUR FABRIC ORDER

SUCCESS! ITEM ADDED TO YOUR BASKET.

⬅ BACK TO PRODUCTS

PRODUCT NAME	QUANTITY	COLOUR	ESTIMATED COST	
Fat Quarters Brights (735)	5 Packs @ £4.95 per pack	Multi	£24.75 (ex. VAT)	✖ Remove

DELIVERY COST: £9.75 *
TOTAL COST: £34.50

YOUR DETAILS

Title:
Mr ▾

Name:

Trading Name:

Phone Number:

Email:

Address Line 1:

Address Line 2:

Town/City:

Post Code:

Delivery Type:
Delivery ▾

* The carriage price quoted does not include VAT and is for delivery to the UK Mainland only.

If you require delivery outside the UK, one of our sales staff will contact you to discuss carriage price when we process your order.

In addition, lengths and prices given are approximate and will be discussed with you before payment is taken for your order.

☐ I agree to the Visage Textiles Terms of Trade
☐ If you DO NOT wish to subscribe to our mailing list, please check this box. Privacy Policy

SEND YOUR REQUEST

The Craft Cotton Company
9-11 Chatley Street
Cheetham Hill
Manchester
M3 1HU

Affiliates   Terms & Conditions   Privacy Policy   Sitemap   © Visage Textiles Limited 2011

Done

www.gameaface.com

www.foolsdoor.com

www.mediatis.ch

Yallee

Yallee | s.m. | Nel linguaggio degli indios Mapuche, pronunciato all'estensione, significa: "Figli degli monti".

TALENTI

Uno dei fondatori di Yallee, al suo primo lavoro, si trovò in un angolo squallido di Milano, seduto davanti a uno dei più esperti e selettivi organizzatori culturali d'Italia – un uomo burbero e geniale. Dopo un colloquio tenutosi a una temperatura da sauna finlandese, quello scopritore di talenti affidò al futuro fondatore di Yallee l'organizzazione di uno dei più importanti festival artistici italiani.

Conosciamo il valore innovativo e spiazzante di chi si affaccia per essere riconosciuto.

Per questo motivo concepiamo Yallee come una bottega d'arte: è un'accademia dove si può imparare il mestiere artigianale e sviluppare il

ABGAR MOURAD'IAN

Discende da industriali del legno del Tavush armeno, emigrati a Yerevan per controllare direttamente gli investimenti in immobili – operazione sospetta all'epoca, ma che aumentò notevolmente il peso finanziario della famiglia Mourad'ian. L'avvento del digitale non ha sorpreso Abgar, che in quel momento si trovava nella Silicon Valley, stagista presso un'azienda poi decotta per via della bolla speculativa. Fonico di avanguardia, Dj Abgar è uno dei protagonisti della scena minimal di Frisco, da dove collabora con noi.

Yallee Srl - PIVA 07147500966

Foto di Nicola De Rosa

Yallee

Yallee | s.m. | Nel linguaggio degli indios Mapuche, pronunciato all'estensione, significa: "Figli degli monti".

Yallee Srl - PIVA 07147500966

Foto di Nicola De Rosa

www.yallee.it

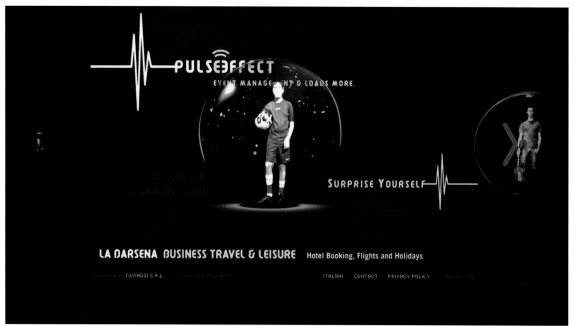

www.pulseeffect.com

www.stellakowalsky.com

www.foolsdoor.com/alaripark-fwa

www.alessiopizzicannella.com

— ARTWORKS / FLAGS

www.guildor.com

GREAT APES

ABOUT · WORK · CURRENT · CONTACT

WE'RE A NATIVE DIGITAL AGENCY

Great Apes is a digital creative agency from Helsinki, Finland. We specialize in providing solutions in both design and development, and our key drivers are creativity, high standards and innovation. We like to think of ourselves as modern-day craftsmen with emphasis on quality over quantity. For us, our work isn't just work – it's what we love to do.

Our services include design and development in virtually all web-centric technologies. We are platform independent and believe in always choosing the right tool for the right job. Everything we do starts with understanding what our client needs – not what seems trendy at the moment.

AUGUST 2011
RISE OF THE APES
We all have now returned from the holidays, rejuvenated and eager for some new challenges.

READ MORE

AUGUST 2011

GREAT APES

ABOUT · WORK · CURRENT · CONTACT

CONTACT

If you would like to know more about how we can help you, don't hesitate to give us a call or drop a few lines of email. We are interested in new opportunities and always looking for that next revolutionary project.

The next time you need a cutting-edge partner, give us a call.

CONTACT US

PHONE
MIKKO SAIRIO, +358-44-3385757

EMAIL
FIRSTNAME.LASTNAME@GREATAPES.FI

ADDRESS
LÖNNROTINKATU 32 D 52, 00180 HELSINKI

VAT ID
2230363-5

LÄÄKELAITOS ESITTÄÄ

VÄÄRENNÖS VAI EI?

RYHDY FILMITÄHDEKSI JA TEE OMA ELOKUVA. VALITSE JOKIN NÄISTÄ KLASSIKOISTA:

LÄÄKEVÄÄRENNÖS ON **RISKI** TERVEYDELLESI.

> KYSYMYKSIÄ JA VASTAUKSIA LÄÄKEVÄÄRENNÖKSISTÄ <
> FRÅGOR OCH SVAR OM FÖRFALSKADE LÄKEMEDEL <

Paras tapa välttää väärennöksiä on hankkia lääkkeet turvallisesti omasta apteekista.

VÄÄRENNETTY LÄÄKE ON VAIKEAMPI TUNNISTAA.

LÄÄKELAITOS
LÄKEMEDELSVERKET
NATIONAL AGENCY
FOR MEDICINES

KUNINGAS KULKUREIDEN

Anna tähdelle kasvot. Valitse hyvä kasvokuva (< 1 Mb) suoraan edestäpäin.
Asettele kuvan silmät ja suu tarkasti ohjainviivojen tasalle.

« PALAA

Skaalaa kuvaa

silmät

suu

Pyöritä kuvaa

KATSO FILMI

Liitä kuva

Liikuta kuvaa

VÄÄRENNETTY LÄÄKE ON VAIKEAMPI TUNNISTAA.

ALKUUN

Paras tapa välttää väärennöksiä on hankkia lääkkeet turvallisesti omasta apteekista.

LÄÄKELAITOS
LÄKEMEDELSVERKET
NATIONAL AGENCY
FOR MEDICINES

laakelaitos.com

Disney.fi   Ankkaprofiili | Rekisteröidy | Ohjeet   ankkatunnuksesi   salasanasi   Sisään

WALT DISNEY

AKU ANKKA

Hae

TIETOLAARI	KIRJASTO	GALLERIA	PELIHALLI	KESKUSTELU	KAUPPA

AKUPEDIA   TOIMITUKSEN BLOGI   ANKKATV   AJANKOHTAISTA

Etusivu > AnkkaTV

Nyt AnkkaTV:ssä!

ANKALLISKANAVA
Tekijähaastatteluja ja dokumentteja

MikkiVisio
Disney-elokuvien trailereita

RoopeRuutu
Ankallisia mainoksia

TaaviTöllö
Disney-elokuvien ekstramateriaalia

ROOPERUUDUSSA NYT:

Näin syntyy Ankka >
Kolmen mestarin terveiset >
Neljän mestarin haastattelu >
Vicarin tervehdys >
Giorgio Cavazzanon
haastattelu 11 / 2007 >
Vicarin haastattelu osa 1 >
Vicarin haastattelu osa 2 >
Vicarin haastattelu osa 3 >

Giorgio Gavanazzon haastattelu 11 / 2007

OHJE

© GYRO GEARLOOSE INC

 AKU ANKKA   AKU ANKAN TASKUKIRJA   ROOPE-SETÄ   lines   AKU ANKKA EKSTRA

www.akuankka.fi

< 60

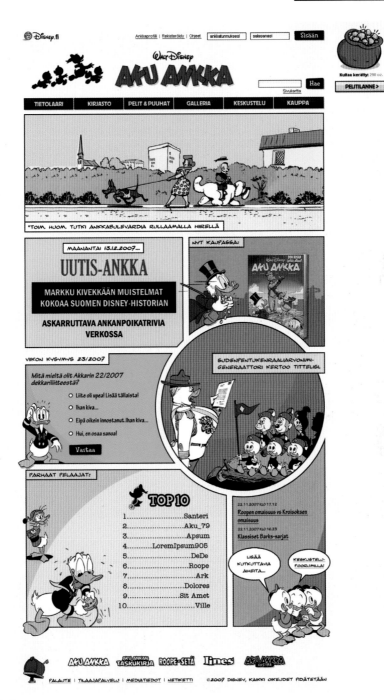

www.akuankka.fi

www.sports-tracker.com

earthcandle.amnesty.org

DAVE PURGAS

DAVE PURGAS | FASHION

www.davepurgas.com

www.nike.com/nikefootball/write-the-future/home?locale=en_GB

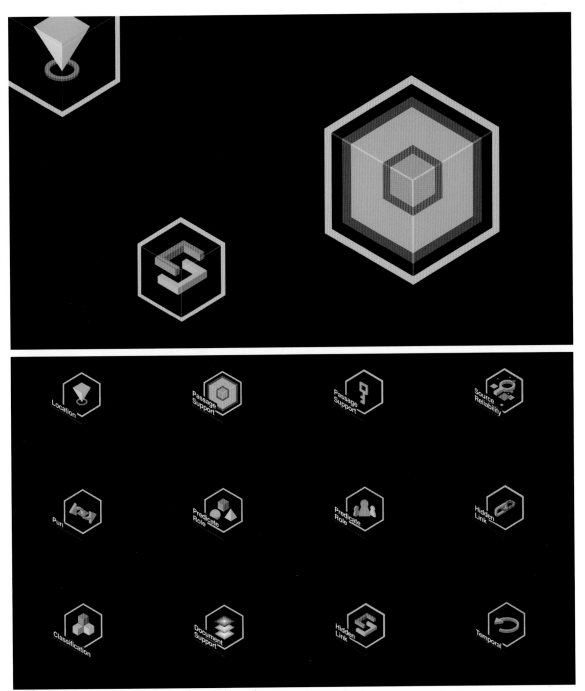

www-03.ibm.com/innovation/us/watson/what-is-watson/science-behind-an-answer.html

www.nike.com/nikefootball/home/?locale=en_GB

109.74.2.129/nike/index.html

www.acumenfund.org/ten

The Bright Future of Car Sharing

A car used to be the ultimate symbol of freedom and independence but increasingly consumers view ownership as an expense and a burden. Often considered the gateway to other forms of Collaborative Consumption, Car Sharing is becoming increasingly popular with its promise of personal convenience and social improvement. It is time to explore this new age where access is better than ownership.

TYPES OF CAR SHARING

P2P

PEER TO PEER

A fleet of cars is owned by a community. The marketplace matches owners of cars that are available to other drivers to rent.

RelayRides   Whipcar   Getaround

BUSINE

A company facilitate the

AUTOMANUFACTURERS

BMW   Peugeot

Zipcar

IN 2009, CAR SHARING DIMINISHED
GLOBAL CARBON DIOXIDE EMISSIONS BY

482,170 Tons

(That's half the weight of the Golden Gate Bridge!)

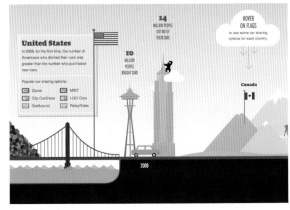

United States

In 2009, for the first time, the number of Americans who ditched their cars was greater than the number who purchased new cars.

Popular car sharing options:

B2C Zipcar	B2C MINT
WP2P City CarShare	WP2P I-GO Cars
P2P GetAround	P2P RelayRides

10 MILLION PEOPLE BOUGHT CARS

14 MILLION PEOPLE GOT RID OF THEIR CARS

HOVER ON FLAGS
to see some car sharing options for each country.

Canada

2009

THE AVERAGE CAR IS USED FOR ONLY ONE HOUR A DAY

Ireland

$715 A MO

www.kirildim.com

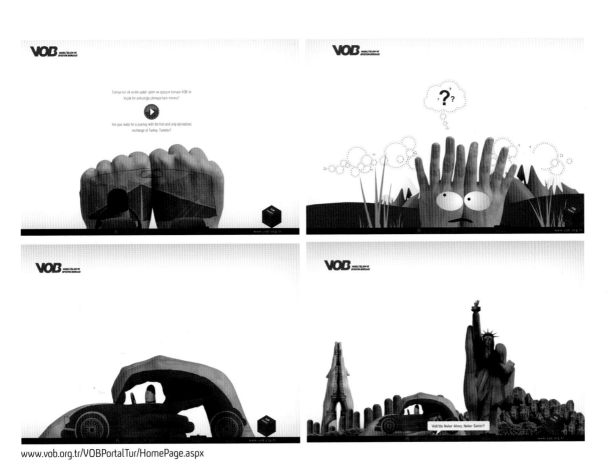

www.vob.org.tr/VOBPortalTur/HomePage.aspx

americansabor.org

www.pbs.org/wgbh/americanexperience/freedomriders

ourmothertongues.org/Home.aspx

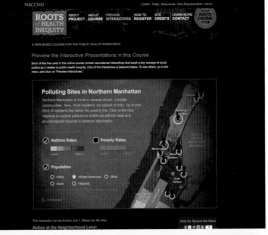

rootsofhealthinequity.org

VISIT THE SPACE

BEN WISCH

Each breath is an opportunity — to embrace life and offer yourself fully into
each moment. If we align ourselves with the natural flow of energy, we can
more easily accept what is and make choices that promote health, well-
being, and balance by using all the lessons and wisdom we've gathered
right up to this present moment.

www.benwisch.com

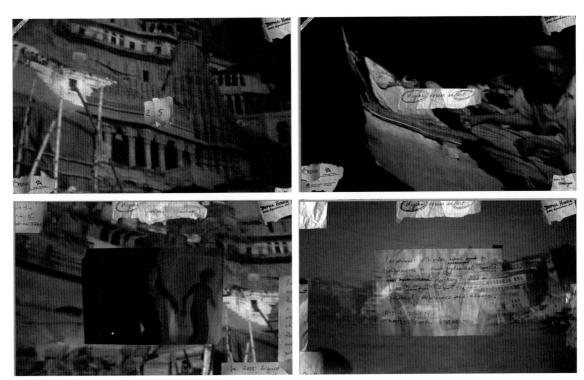

www.dipnahorra.com

www.garyandrewpoole.com/archive/experience/red-grange

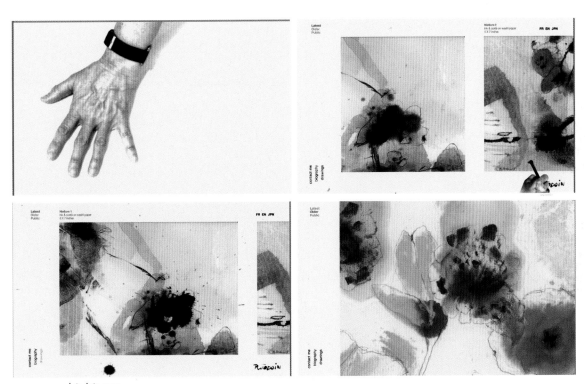

www.raymondejodoin.com

www.knoed.com

www.826seattle.org

www.knoed.com

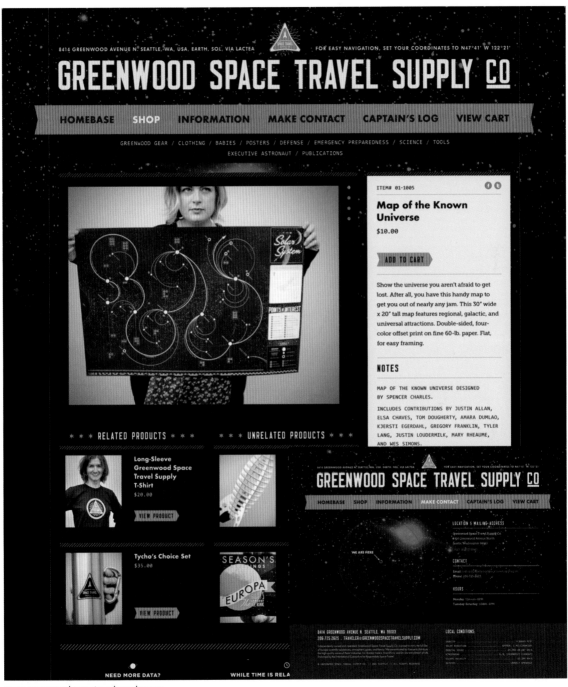

www.greenwoodspacetravelsupply.com

83 >

Home / Shop / FAQs / About / Gallery / Contact

Cart   0 Items | $0.00

VIEW CART   CHECKOUT

Shop

Chicago Brown Mens
$20.00

Chicago Brown Womens
$20.00

Chicago Red Mens
$20.00

Chicago Red Womens
$20.00

Home / Shop / FAQs / About / Gallery / Contact

Cart   0 Items | $0.00

VIEW CART   CHECKOUT

About

If you know Chicago, you know the 'L'. And now you can wear it.

In Chicago, we call our transit train system 'The L.' This t-shirt collection is based on the current CTA 'L' signage, which is a modification of the original 1969 design, known as the "Kennedy-Dan Ryan" signage, set in Helvetica and color-coded to match the eight corresponding CTA 'L' lines. See the gallery.

Chicago pride is induced by the kinship we feel with our neighborhoods and the transit lines that connect them. That sense of pride, coupled with our affection for typography and design, have inspired us to create this series of transit t-shirts (also known as L-Shirts).

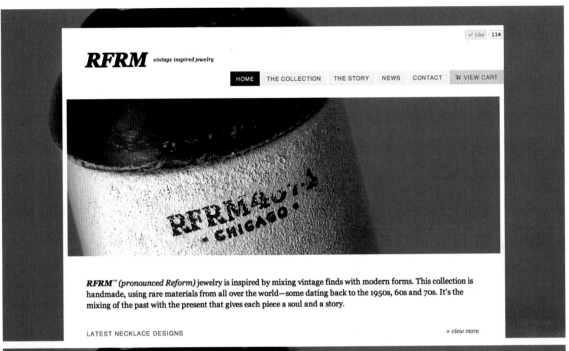

RFRM™ *(pronounced Reform)* jewelry is inspired by mixing vintage finds with modern forms. This collection is handmade, using rare materials from all over the world—some dating back to the 1950s, 60s and 70s. It's the mixing of the past with the present that gives each piece a soul and a story.

LATEST NECKLACE DESIGNS   » view more

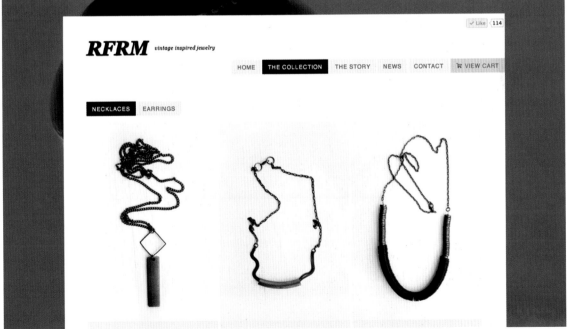

rfrmjewelry.com

www.kooba.ie
www.rubystarmobile.com

www.kooba.ie

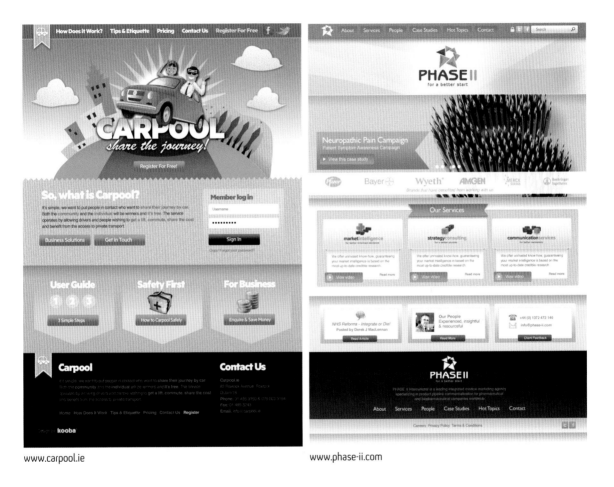

www.carpool.ie

www.phase-ii.com

www.marketingsociety.ie

www.sparkqual.com

www.revealireland.ie

aitan.com

dimpus.com.br

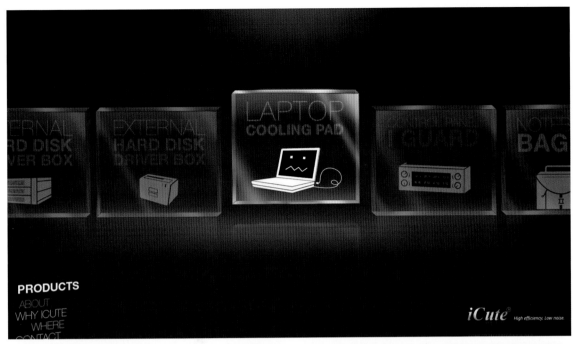

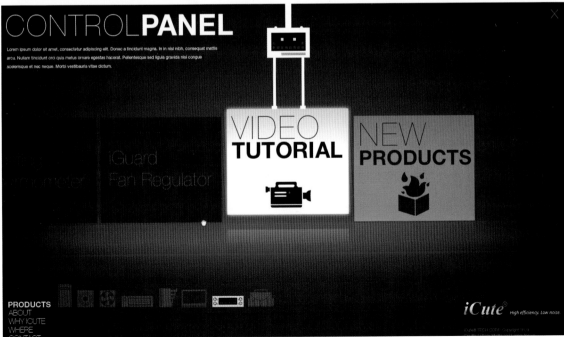

www.icute.com.tw/en

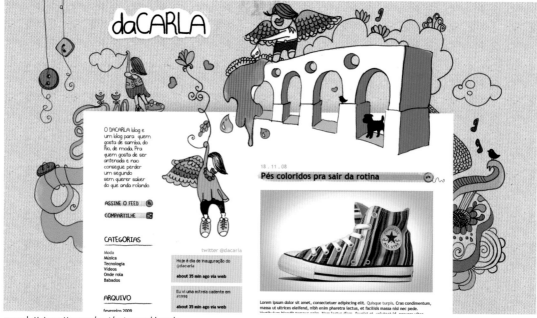

www.leticiamotta.com/port/category/dacarla

telecine.globo.com

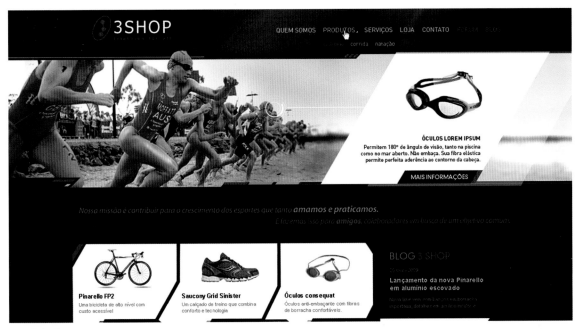

www.3shopbr.com

www.leticiamotta.com/port/category/oito-oito

www.lotie.com

www.lotie.com

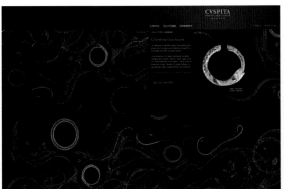

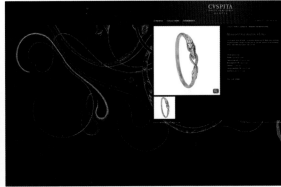

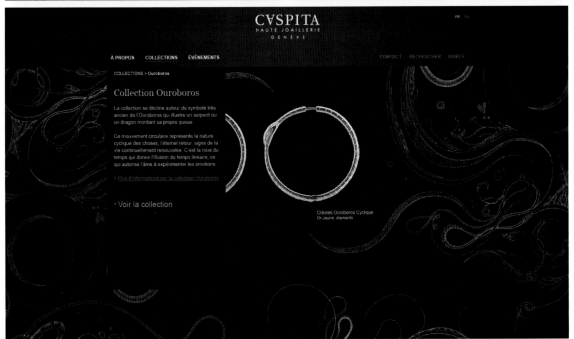

Collection Ouroboros

La collection se décline autour du symbole très ancien de l'Ouroboros qui illustre un serpent ou un dragon mordant sa propre queue.

Ce mouvement circulaire représente la nature cyclique des choses, l'éternel retour, signe de la vie continuellement renouvelée. C'est la roue du temps qui donne l'illusion du temps linéaire, ce qui autorise l'âme à expérimenter les émotions.

· Plus d'informations sur la collection Ouroboros

· Voir la collection

Créoles Ouroboros Cyclique
Or Jaune, diamants

en.caspita.ch/collections/ouroboros

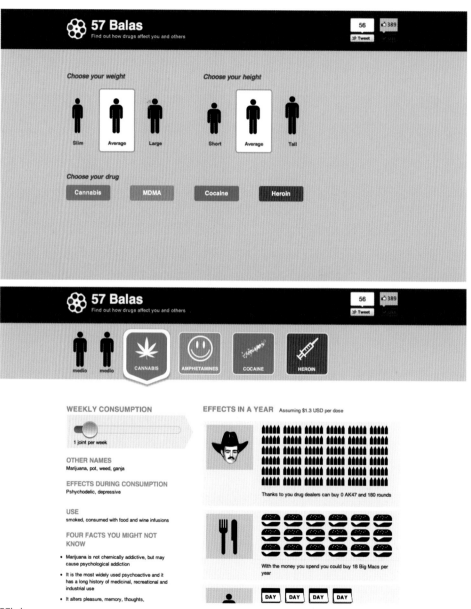

57balas.com

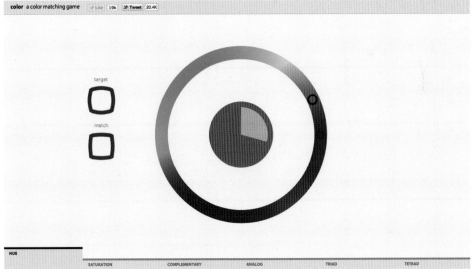

www.color.method.ac

Bullshiter
Bullshiter es el generador de bullshit definitivo.

Inspírame

Su bullshit AQUÍ

Bullshiter es una tontería de **inefable** y **doctoraw**

Bullshiter
Bullshiter es el generador de bullshit definitivo.

Inspírame

Sin embargo, no hemos de olvidar que la consulta con los numerosos militantes cumple deberes importantes en la determinación de toda una serie de criterios ideológicamente sistematizados en un frente común de actuación regeneradora.

Bullshiter es una tontería de **inefable** y **doctoraw**

bullshiter.inefable.net

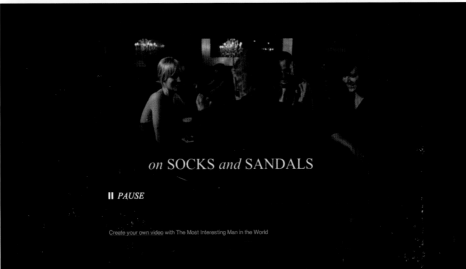

interestingman.in

INSIDE MASSIVE

Controlled insanity,
with lots of sun
and a sea view.

PT EN   GET OUR NEWSLETTER   FOLLOW US!

MASSIVE
DIGITAL CREATIVE AGENCY

WE MAKE INSPIRATIONAL BRANDS COME ALIVE THROUGH INNOVATION AND PERFECTIONISM

MASSIVE NEWS

THE ART OF LIVING TIME
18.11.2011

Massive developed the portal for the new magazine "Turbilhão", launched by Tempus Distribuição.

MASSIVE SOTD BY AWWWARDS
28.10.2011

This nomination by the distinguished international community turns Massive into the only Portuguese company to date with three of these awards.

MASSIVE WINS SILVER AT SAPO AWARDS
28.10.2011

Massive was recognized at Sapo Awards 2011, which acknowledge online creativity in several areas, with the project "Graça Viterbo Interior Design".

MASSIVE IN BRIEFING
22.09.2011

The launch of our new site made news across the media. Read the Briefing piece here.

3 YEARS ROCKING
15.09.2011

Time goes by fast and we've already turned 3. We are very proud of our work and its recognition.

SELECTED PROJECTS

FLUENCE CAMPAIGN
Renault Fluence
DETAILS →

7 PORTUGUESE WONDERS IN THE WORLD
DETAILS →

NESPRESSO PORTUGAL
Nespresso Flavours
DETAILS →

AGENCY ACTIVITY

I WANT TO WORK HERE

If you have the skills and the talent to develop benchmark projects, Massive is the place for you!

JOIN US

KEEP IN TOUCH

The spam you can't lose.

E–MAIL

SITE MAP
Home   The Agency
Services   Portfolio
News   Contacts

ADDRESS
Av. Marginal, Ed. Parque Oceano, 4º
Santo Amaro de Oeiras
2780–322 Oeiras - Portugal

OUR CONTACTS
tel.   + 351 214 544 545
fax.   + 351 214 544 549
mail   info@itsmassive.com

MASSIVE
Digital Creative Agency

HOME   COMPANY   SERVICES   PROJECTS   BOOKS   LIFESTYLE   NEWS   PRESS

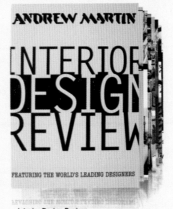

Interior Design Review
Available through Graça Viterbo Interior Design

www.gviterbo.com

nlengenharia.com

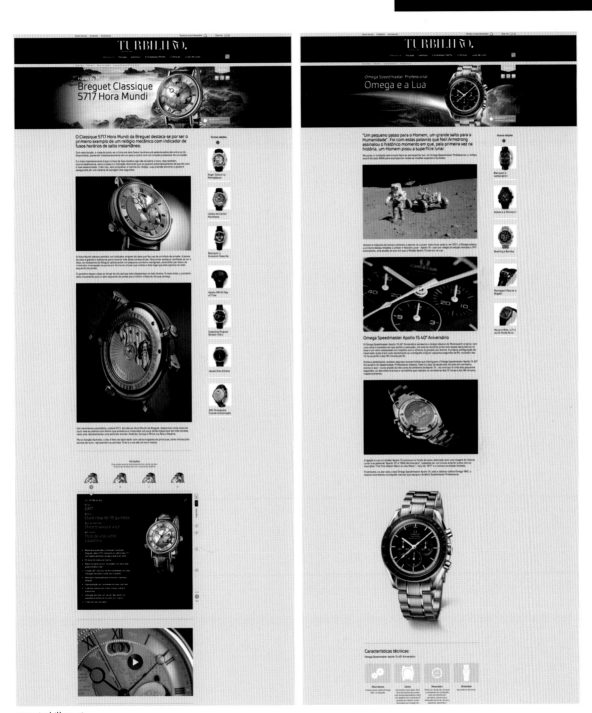

www.turbilhao.pt

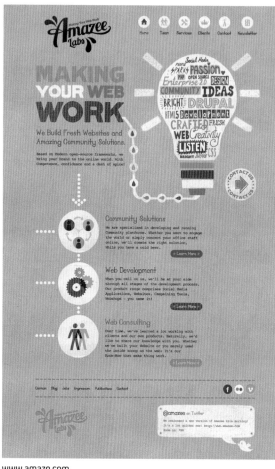

www.amaze.com

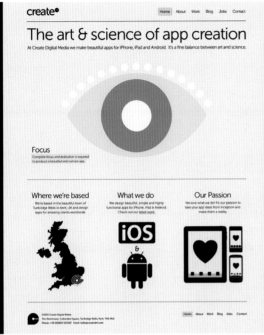

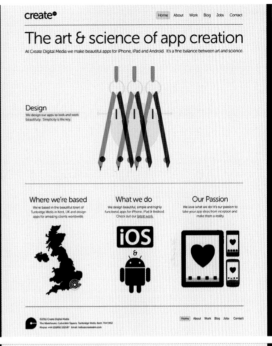

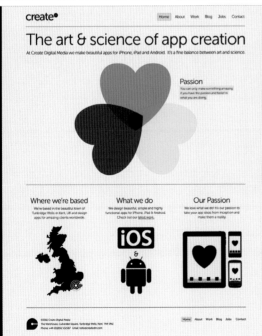

createdm.com

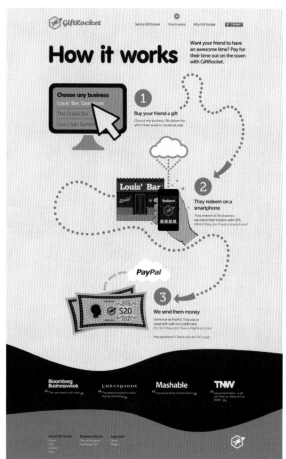

www.giftrocket.com

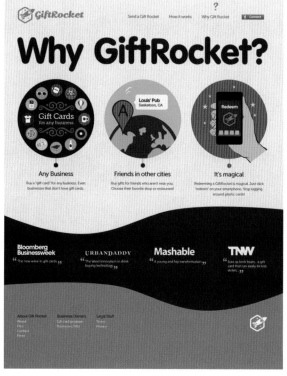

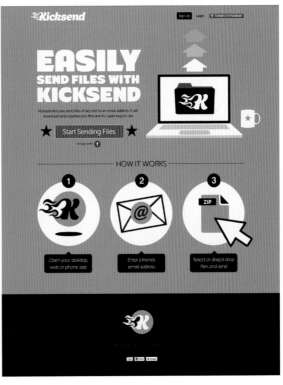

kicksend.com

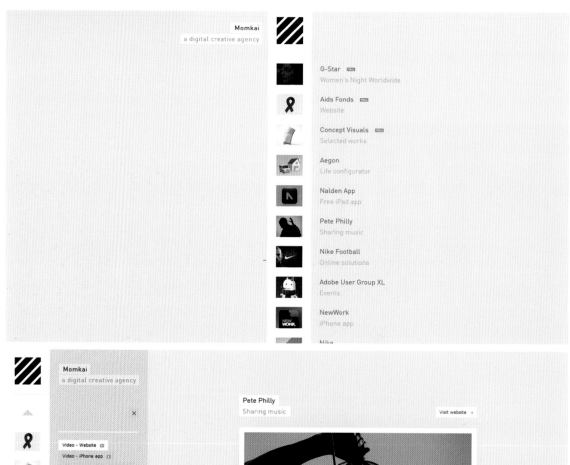

Momkai
a digital creative agency

G-Star
Women's Night Worldwide

Aids Fonds
Website

Concept Visuals
Selected works

Aegon
Life configurator

Nalden App
Free iPad app

Pete Philly
Sharing music

Nike Football
Online solutions

Adobe User Group XL
Events

NewWork
iPhone app

Nike

Momkai
a digital creative agency

×

Video - Website
Video - iPhone app
Video - Facebook integration
Interface
Interface
Interface
Interface
Sharing
Upcoming Track
Upcoming Track
Menu navigation
About
Track overview
Downloads

Facebook
Facebook
Facebook

iPhone app 1
iPhone app 2

Pete Philly
Sharing music

Visit website →

About the project	What we did	Year
Critically acclaimed music artist Pete Philly and Momkai met last year to discuss the creation of a new, unique experience for his fans - one in which he releases a new track and accompanying video every week for 14 weeks. The approach was A) to use the power of sharing (via Facebook, Twitter, Vimeo, email, YouTube, downloads, and an iPhone app) to make everyone aware of his new solo music plus showcase his performance and B) to let the audience focus by adding just one track every week and accompanying each track with a super slowmo hi-resolution video.	Video script & concept Concept Concept design Functional design Interface design Technical realisation Animation Art direction Visualization Video production Mimoto CMS 3.3	2010 2009

NOVEMBER 4TH, 2011

RSVP FOR THIS NIGHT

WOMEN'S NIGHT

www.g-star.com

www.nalden.net

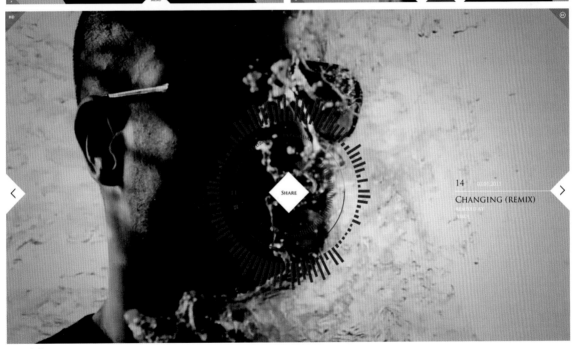

petephilly.com

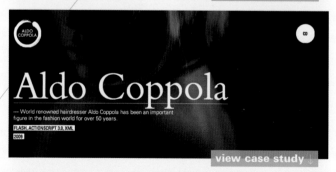

VISION

one world, one reason unchanging, one vision

17th January 2012
Fashion Diary 2012

VISION

« » positions: female

www.visionmanichini.it

20calendars.lavazza.com

20calendars.lavazza.com

www.bokicabo.com

www.bokicabo.com

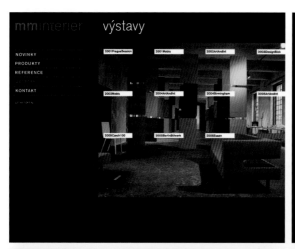

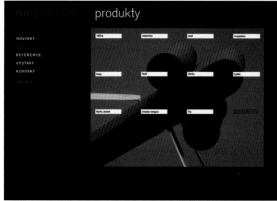

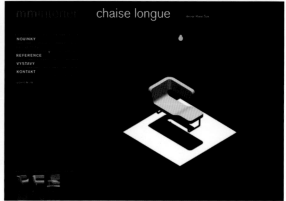

www.mminterier.cz

www.ookidoo.com/cz

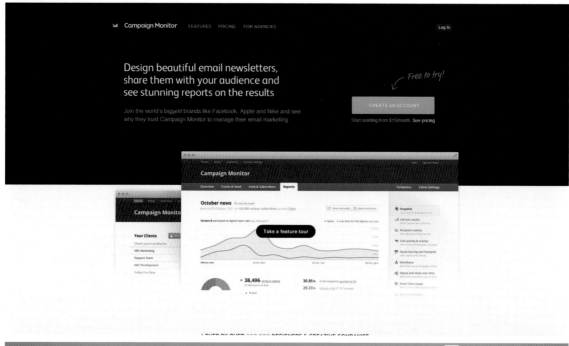

Beautiful reports

Simply stunning!

For every campaign you send, we provide a beautiful set of real-time reports allowing you to go beyond opens, and measure your campaign's social activity, sales and ROI.

RECIPIENT ACTIVITY

Who opens your campaigns, when and how many times. Using our tools, drill right down and see each user's activity

FORWARDS

Track viral activity by seeing exactly which subscribers forward on to a friend

BOUNCES

See who bounced and why, and we'll figure out if we should try again or remove

SHARES

See not only which subscribers are sharing with their friends, but what they're saying about you on Twitter and Facebook

www.campaignmonitor.com

Log In

Prevue is a concept sharing app.

It's a simple and elegant tool that allows you to upload and share your work. It's used by designers, studios and freelance creatives all over the world to privately share work with clients.

Create a free account

Our whole studio uses it and I know our clients love it. It's actually changed the way we work massively for the better.

Prevue like fine wine, it just keeps getting better!

Image Mechanics

Jamie Young, Designer - Provokateur

Designer → Client

Present designs to your clients in a clean and easy-to-use interface that allows your work to speak for itself.

- Add your own branding
- 100% ad-free
- Cloud hosted & lightning fast
- Customise the page style for each upload

Either send your clients an individual image, or group your work together into projects. If you're looking for feedback, your client can even add comments and annotations.

I love this scarf! — Prevue

Home
Add to project
Account
Settings

 Built for you

Built for freelancers and studios, Prevue has everything you need to quickly and professionally share designs with clients

🔒 **Privacy**

For sensitive work, you're able to password protect your projects. Only clients with access can view your designs

 Get feedback

With the click of a button, you can allow clients to comment on your projects, and annotate on single images

⚙ **Your own brand**

Add your own logo on all the pages that are publically shared with your clients. Treat the app as your studio's own tool

Sound good? Sign up

Log In
Support & FAQ
Our Blog

Twitter @prevueit
Like us on Facebook
Take a Tour

Terms

prevue.it

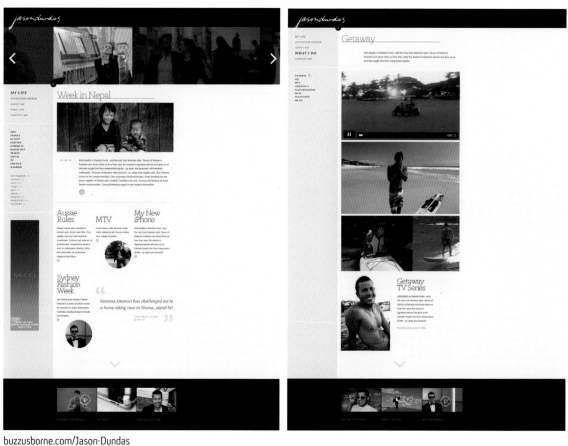

buzzusborne.com/Jason-Dundas

www.rangowhackandwin.com.au

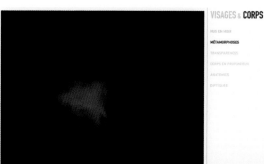

edepazzi.com

www.edepazzi.com/visagescorps.html

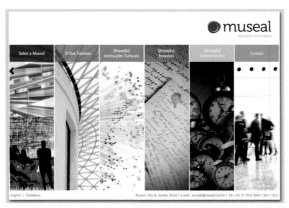

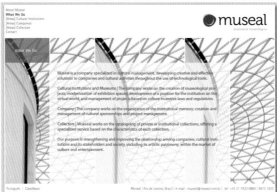

www.museal.com.br/intro.html

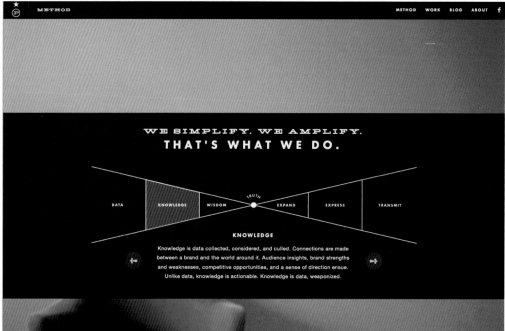

planetpropaganda.com

1world2wheels.org

www.duluthtrading.com

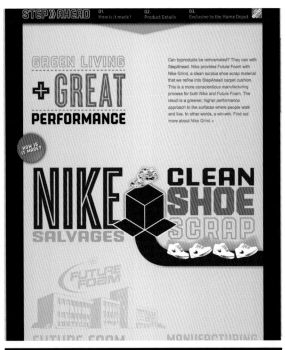

www.stepaheadcushion.com

DESIGNER.
MARKETER.
MOTION
GRAPHER.
PLANNER.
DEVELOPEr.
EXPERIENCE

EXPERIENCE
PEOPLE

SAMSUNG
DEVELOPER
DAY 2012 AT MWC

Plus X
Creative
Partner

Plus MX
Creative
Mobile Developing
Company

HOME
EXPERIENCE
PEOPLE
/ GALLERY

Plus X
Creative Partner

www.cgv.co.kr

raffaelstueken.de

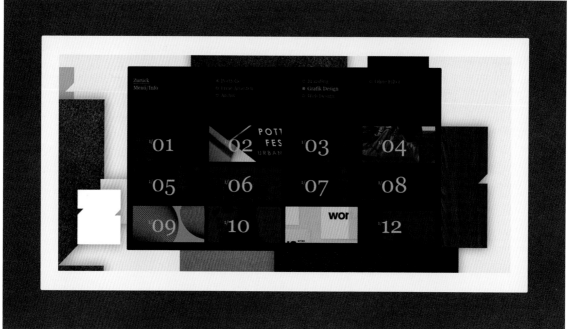

raffaelstueken.de

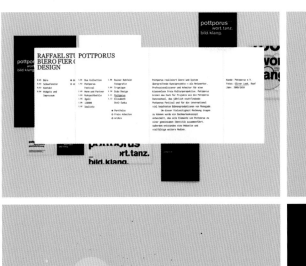
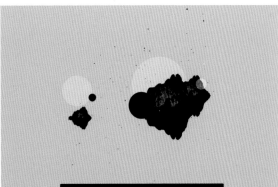
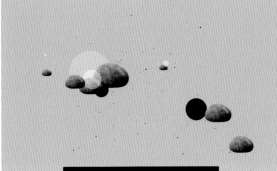

raffaelstueken.de

www.redtiki.com.au

www.luhsetea.com

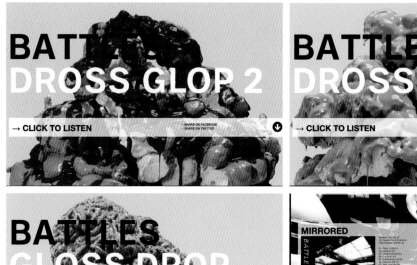

BATTLES
DROSS GLOP 2

→ **CLICK TO LISTEN**   → SHARE ON FACEBOOK
→ SHARE ON TWITTER

BATTLES
DROSS GLOP 1

→ **CLICK TO LISTEN**   → SHARE ON FACEBOOK
→ SHARE ON TWITTER

BATTLES
GLOSS DROP

→ ITUNES / → AMAZON / → BLEEP   → SHARE ON FACEBOOK
→ JB HI-FI / → FNAC / → BTTLS STORE / →LIVE DATES   → SHARE ON TWITTER

MIRRORED   → SHARE ON FACEBOOK
→ SHARE ON TWITTER

bttls.com

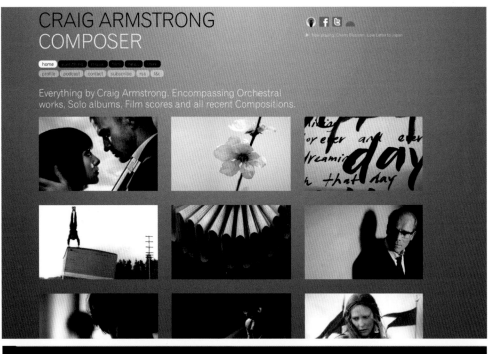

craigarmstrong.com

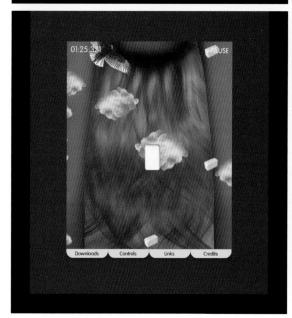

butterstargalactica.hudsonmohawke.com

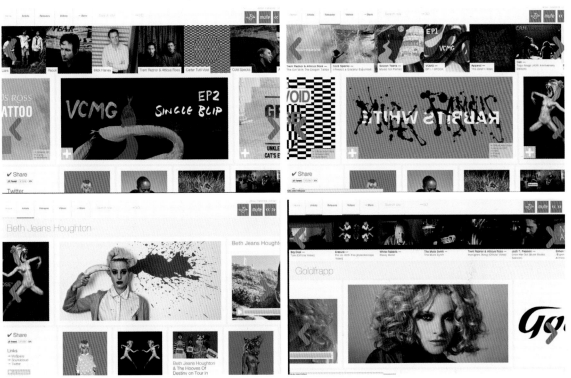

mute.com

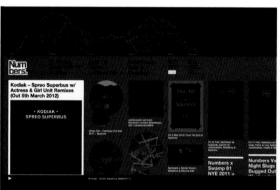

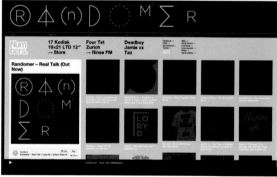

nmbrs.net

www.upsdfektmlm.com

warp.net

We create
DIGITAL
EXPERIENCES

rtraction is a digital agency interested
in positive change - *creating* it, *learning* it,
influencing it, and helping our clients *navigate* it.

rtraction
2011 Holiday eCard

In this year's holiday e-card, we took
the opportunity to show our
appreciation for our clients, support
a local initiative near to our hearts
and commemorate our...

Childreach
A Sneak Peek

A nonprofit organization dedicated
to early childhood development is
relaunching its site to better engage
families and the community...

Harrison Pensa
Website

A local law firm makes a bold move
with its new website, showing off its
innovative side with a fresh design
and a more personal look at its ...

Season's Greetings

[Let it snow...]

rtraction 2011 holiday card

To celebrate the season, our e-card let our
clients, friends and fans scroll to stroll
through a winter wonderland and reveal our
gift to our supporters and our community:
100 trees purchased in support of ReForest
London's Million Tree Challenge! For those
who are snow globe fans—and who
isn't?—we displayed an animated snow
globe at the end of the journey.

View E-card

ABOUT   WORK   PROCESS   TEAM   BLOG   CONTACT

CANADA'S
WORST
CHARITY WEBSITE

Come on Canada!

MARCH 6
IN INTIMIDATE AD FORTIS

VOTING   OPENS

Learn More

aeolianhall.ca

milliontrees.ca

seymourpowell

**case studies
the company
news and press
contact us**

photography and design
strategy and NPD
product design
structural design
graphic design
transport

+44(0)20 7381 6433
design@seymourpowell.com

Nokia
C-Armor fashion concepts

**Designing ahead of
the curve**

1   case study

2   images

3   printable version

seymourpowell

**case studies
the company
news and press
contact us**

about us
what we do
our vision
join the team

"Seymourpowell has brought real expertise and has been a catalyst
in our thinking about the future role of the product and how we can
better express our brands through the design of innovative
products."
Keith Weed, Vice President, Unilever

Seymourpowell is one of the world's leading design and innovation
companies.

Founded in 1984 by Richard Seymour and Dick Powell, the London-
based group of award-winning designers has produced some of the
milestone products of the last two decades. The company is now
part of the Loewy Group.

Seymourpowell is currently 80 people, combining a design studio,
research centre, materials library and prototyping workshop.

Companies from around the world come to us because they need to
answer three questions. What should we sell? Why should we do it?
How do we do it? We provide the answers to those questions
through, design innovation, transportation design, ethnographic user
research, strategy and new product development (NPD), trends and
forecasting, product design and development, 3D structural design
and 2D graphic design.

We have a unique holistic approach to design and innovation, which
combines in-depth experience and up to date intelligence about
people, markets and businesses. We have the ability to forecast and
interpret the vital implications of behaviours and work out future
scenarios to give our clients the confidence and reassurance they are
making the right decision.

We are skilled in exploiting ideas that create real value and always
look to move clients forward creatively. We are not just visionary
thinkers, but future doers. Ultimately, we are about making things
better: better for people, better for business and better for the world.

Seymourpowell Limited is a limited liability company registered in
England and Wales. Registered Office: 1st Floor, 59 Park Street,
London, SE1 9EQ Registered No: 01845134.

+44(0)20 7381 6433
info@seymourpowell.com

seymourpowell

**case studies
the company
news and press
contact us**

+44(0)20 7381 6433
design@seymourpowell.com

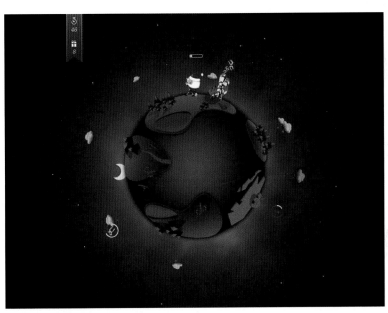

www.checklandkindleysides.com/santa-goes-solo

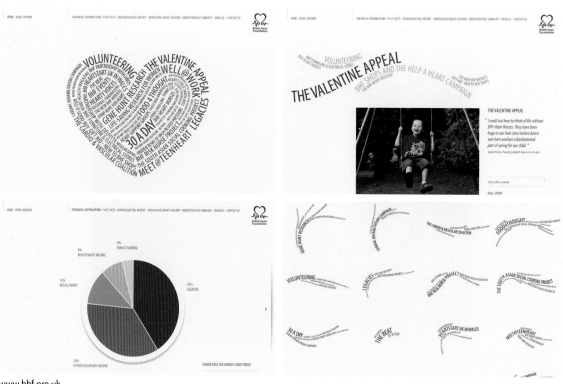

about
news
portfolio
creative knowledge
contact

checkland kindleysides

Tel: +44 (0) 116 2644 700
Fax: +44 (0) 116 2644 701
Email: claire@checklandkindleysides.com

about
news
portfolio
creative knowledge
contact

the company
what we do
the people
join us

On one level Checkland Kindleysides is a multidisciplinary design studio. Among other things we define strategy, create brand identities, retail environments, exhibitions, in-store merchandising and graphic communications. Whatever the brief, we are committed to working alongside our clients to answer it in the most beneficial and effective way for business.

On another level, however, we don't like to be pigeonholed quite so readily. Our years of practical experience mean that there's more to this design studio than most.

Perhaps the biggest point of difference is our considerable on-site workshop. What once began back in 1979 as a workbench – a place to draw and make, has over the years developed into a great resource where skilled craftsmanship freely informs the design process.

about
news
portfolio
creative knowledge
contact

31/03/2010
Levi's flagship store, London

Levi's Flagship store on Regent St. has opened today.

It is a place where craftsmanship and authenticity deliver the most genuine experience of the brand.

Click to Levi's in our portfolio section for more images.

08/07/2009
Converse at Bread & Butter Berlin

Converse's latest B&B exhibition took place in a hanger at Berlin's Tempelhof airport. The stand's exterior was emblazoned with posters from the current 'music moments' campaign, while inside nine ranges are depicted via 'spark of creativity' imagery from A/W 09/10. We used the latest campaign to inspire the design of each product were brand around music, fashion, art and sport, creating product stories to present the ranges.

12/03/2009
Chain Store Age Award

Following on from all the positive press about our Timberland store at Westfield, the project has received the accolade of 'Best Store Exterior' from the US's Chain Store Age – Retail Store of the Year Awards.

The striking façade is a contemporary interpretation of the Timberland identity and makes this store a landmark site within the centre.

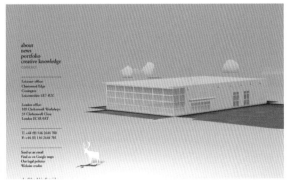

about
news
portfolio
creative knowledge
contact

Leicester office:
Charnwood Edge
Cossington
Leicestershire LE7 4UZ

London office:
109 Clerkenwell Workshops
31 Clerkenwell Close
London EC1R 0AT

T: +44 (0) 116 2644 700
F: +44 (0) 116 2644 701

Send us an email
Find us on Google maps
Our legal policies
Website credits

www.checklandkindleysides.com

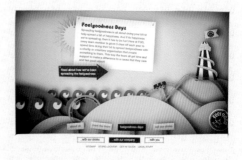

www.feelgooddrinks.co.uk

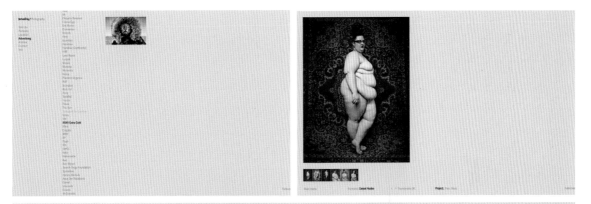

jamesdayphoto.com

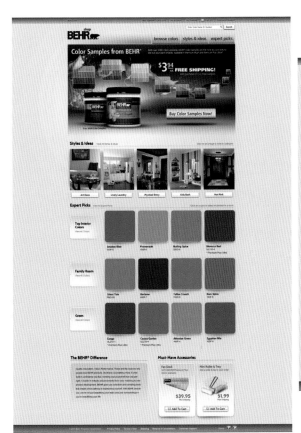

www.behr.com/Behr/home

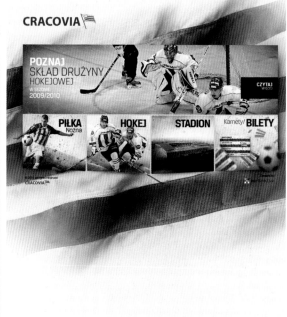

cracovia.pl

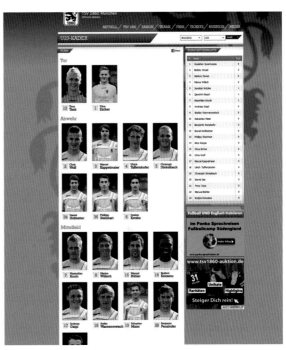

www.tsv1860.de

www.nespresso.com/kazaar

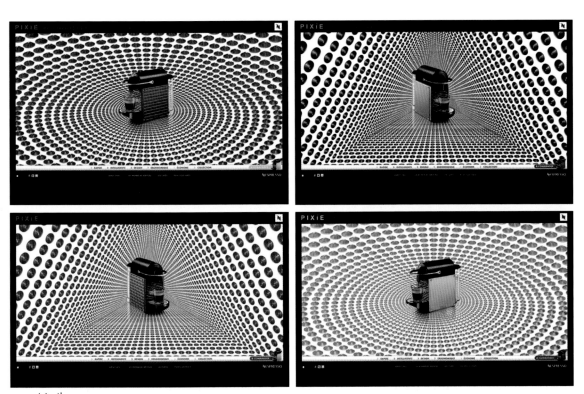

www.pixieathome.com

collection.gasjeans.com

projects.thinkingabout.it/gas/denim_ss11

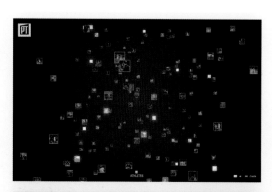

www.protalent.it

www.thinkingabout.it/subdomains/projects/refrigiwear

So, having studied photography... oh wait, as if you care. In these days of High-Dynamic-Range, über-pixel, ISO-infinity super-shallow-bokeh™ ...this page represents just another amatuer dabbling foray into silver halide

www.thismanslife.co.uk

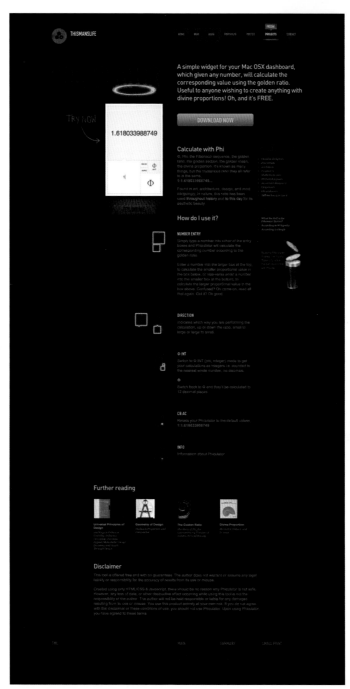

ROMAN VRTISKA — ARCHITECTURE +
GRAPHIC DESIGN +
PRODUCT DESIGN +

roman-vrtiska.com

HRISTINA GEORGIEVSKA

CONTACT•BIO   REFERENCE

BEAUTY
FASHION
AD'S & MOTION
CAMPAIGNS

ce Vita — Make up foto © Anka Horvacic   Dolce Vita — Make up foto © Anka Horvacic   Dolce Vita — Make up foto © Anka Horvacic

www.hristinageorgievska.com

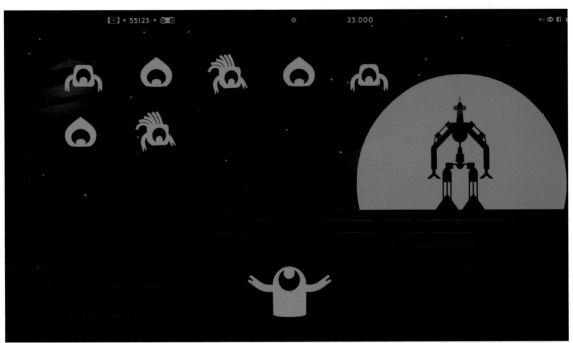

the-planet-zero.com

www.forgetmenot.tv

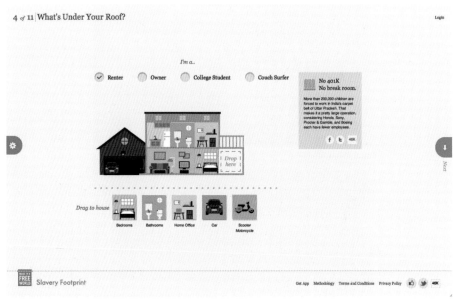

slaveryfootprint.org

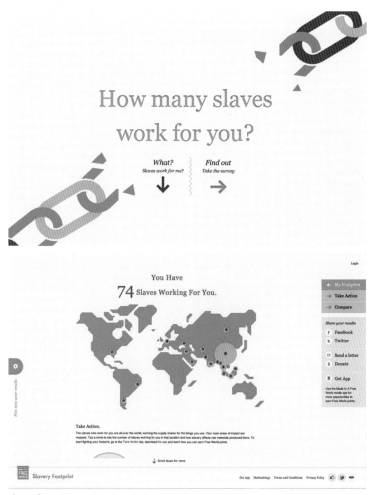

slaveryfootprint.org

www.diesel.com/eyewear

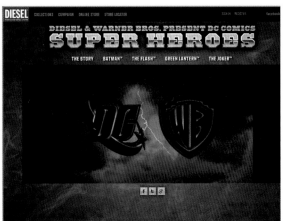

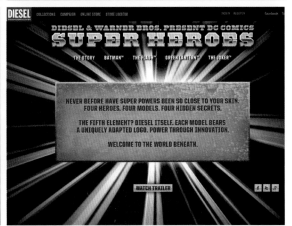

www.diesel.com/freshandbright

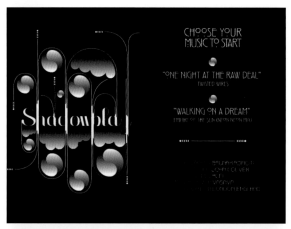

Shadowplay

CHOOSE YOUR
MUSIC TO START

"ONE NIGHT AT THE RAW DEAL"
TWISTED WIRES

"WALKING ON A DREAM"
EMPIRE OF THE SUN (NEON NEON MIX)

www.hintmag.com

www.mango.com

173 >

es.tous.com/tous/en/manolo-for-tous/home

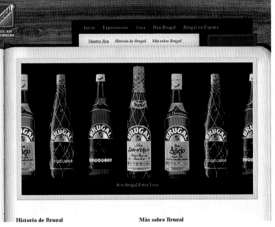

EL POLO MAGNÉTICO

Fecha: 13 julio 2009 · **Tags:** ruta

De camino por la Ruta44, una preciosa carretera que acompaña el mar durante varios kilómetros al sur de República Dominicana, decidimos comprobar si el Polo Magnético es realmente una maravilla de la física o una simple ilusión óptica. Leer más

Fecha

Clasificar por:

Última semana
Último mes
Todo

SOY DOMINICANO, SOY OPTIMISTA
13 septiembre 2009

RUTA ARTÍSTICA
13 septiembre 2009

Y CUANDO SALGA LA LUNA...
13 septiembre 2009

ODA AL ZAPATO PLANO INEXISTENTE
9 septiembre 2009

EL SURFITO
7 septiembre 2009

EL RÍO MÁS CORTO DEL MUNDO
5 septiembre 2009

ARTISTA DE LARGO

Ron Brugal Extra Viejo

Historia de Brugal   Más sobre Brugal

www.brugal-ron.com

www.glingglo.net

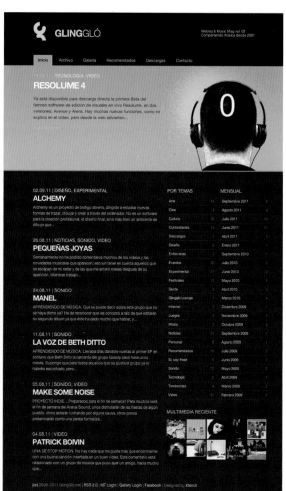

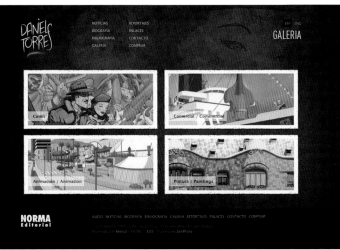

www.torresdaniel.com

www.artesanio.com

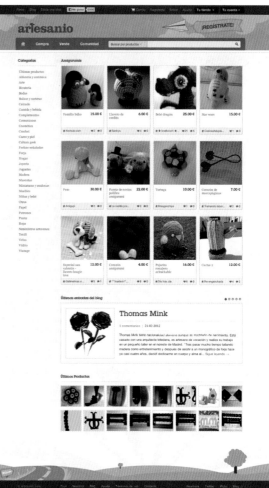

www.xtencil.com

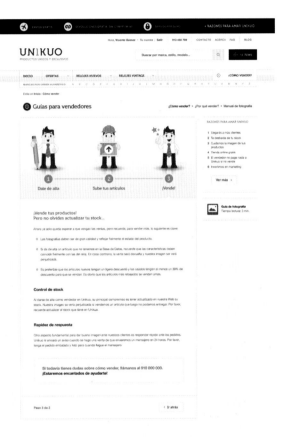

www.unikuo.com

179 >

www.trabattoni.com

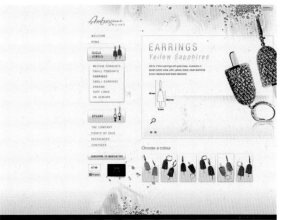

www.ambrosinimilano.com

www.xavier-k.com

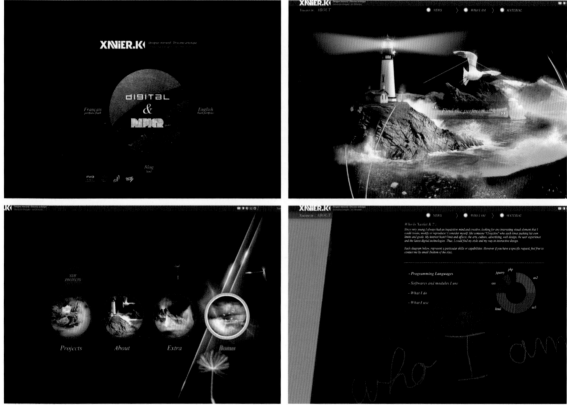

www.xavier-k.com/en

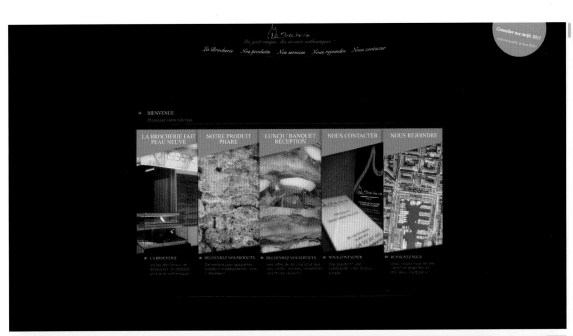

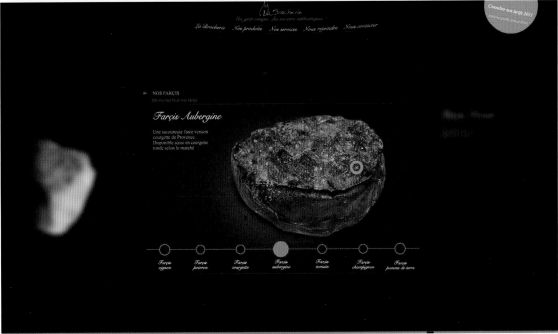

www.labrocherienice.com

yípori

Home
Downloads
Characters
Blog
Shop

Water Coast Wallpaper

Take a cool dip under the sea with Smoole and Pip as they investigate a rather pointy creature floating around the sea. Don't get too close guys! New wallpaper available, get it now!

extra, extra, read all about it

Desktop Wallpapers

Latest News

Latest happenings in the world of Yipori. New projects, artwork and latest breakfast cereal news!

Questions? Answers!

Want to know what makes Yipori tick? Got a question of deep intellectual worth? (Or just want to know what Yipori thinks about rocket powered turtles) This is the place to visit.

Gallery Now Open

Become a fan

facebook

About

Yipori is made by Chris Alexander, an euthusatic illustrator and web developer based in Cirencester in the Cotswolds. He has a passion for creating cute and happy characters with a definate 'kawaii' slant. **More...**

Twitter

Smoole and the Pip fish investigate a rather pointy creature floating around the sea. http://t.co/dNFckIVF aka new wallpaper available now! 45 minutes ago

Happy Valentines Day http://t.co/P2Fg9Jan This little Inkmallow is looking for someone special :) 8 days ago

@happy_food Yes! Look forward to seeing that one. 32 days ago

Contact

Do you need to know something about the characters, the creator, or just want to say hi? We would love to hear from you. **More...**

Copyright ©2012 - Yipori

www.yipori.com

yoke

- Work
- Services
- About us
- Contact us
- Blog

WE LIKE CHANGE

WE ARE A SMALL DESIGN STUDIO

DOING GREAT THINGS FOR GOOD PEOPLE

Our Story

"Design is something that we love doing so why not do it for a cause that we feel worthy"

Yoke was founded by Jay Bigford and Alister Wynn. It was formed with the idea that our day job should not just be a means to earn our keep, but also an extension of our values that we keep close to our heart. This was the premise for Yoke.

alisterwynn.co.uk
jaybigford.com

Yoke is also built on strong foundations from years of experience in the digital industry and working with some of the UK's best creative agencies, on a whole host global brands like Orange, Nokia, Disney and O2.

 Claire Rosling – wordsmith and smiley face, assisting in the smooth running of Yoke Towers.

All the character illustration for this site was done by our talented friend Wei Ong, also known as Silent Hobo.

Our Approach

We see life and work as interconnected, we must be happy at work and to do this we have to apply the same values to all areas of our lives. There are 3 main driving forces behind this approach.

Community
"As a whole we are greater than the sum of our parts."

Show more

Creativity
"We are creative people and that doesn't stop when we leave the studio"

Show more

Collaboration
"When a project begins we like to think that we become an integral part of your team, not you becoming our 'client'."

Show more

Our ethics

Humans are a busy bunch of people and our combined activity is slowly taking its toll on our little planet.

Being the only home we have, we feel that we want to contribute to a shift in behaviour so that our planet, its people and creatures can continue to live here in relative harmony. What this means is using our resources more intelligently and making sure that everyone is given a fairer deal. We strongly believe this can be done which is why we want to work with those that have made a choice to lessen their impact on society and the world and contribute to positive change. We feel that as a digital agency the biggest impact we can make is exercising this choice and ensuring that our creativity finds a good home. Of course we do the little things as well like fueling ourselves with fairtrade organic coffee.

Creative Contribution

As part of this selective work ethic we operate a Creative Contribution policy. We offer our services to people or organisations we think are really trying to do something positive with their energies. We offer them without charge in order to help them to achieve their goals without the financial burden usually associated with our industry. Many smaller organisations do not have the budget to afford online marketing services and usually go without this channel of communication and outreach. For small charities and NGOs the internet provides a limitless source of fundraising and exposure potential, the like of which could not be afforded using traditional marketing methods. Our aim is to take our extensive knowledge and skills and help these organisations by giving them the tools they require to exploit this potential channel.

Contact Us

Take a look at what's going on

RECENT RUMBLINGS

Zero Waste Events
CMS, PROJECT, SUSTAINABILITY, WEBSITES

Campaign website to make the London 2012 Olympic Games Zero-Landfill.

Read more

Yoke invited as resident thinkers on Nowhereisland
ARTS & DESIGN, BRISTOL, NEWS

If we were to create a new nation, how might we begin?

Read more

Can you afford to make your work socially responsible?
BUSINESS, SUSTAINABILITY

We explore how you can make your ethical dreams a reality.

Read more

Yoke's story so far…
NEWS

8 weeks in, we take a look back at what's been going on and what has worked for us.

Read more

Too Good To Waste
CMS, YOKE, PROJECT, WEBSITE

Campaign website to reduce food waste in restaurants.

Read more

Successful social media campaigns we 'like'
CHARITIES

Social media is the campaigner's new best friend

Read more

Organic Farming
BRANDING, CMS, FARMING & FOOD, PROJECT, WEBSITES

Making life easier for an Organic Farming Research and Education Centre

Read more

The multiscreen world and responsive design
ARTS & DESIGN, MOBILE, SCIENCE & TECH

The landscape is changing, make sure your site is ready.

Read more

What we do
CRAFTING EXPERIENCES

Here at yoke we spend our time creating, designing and building experiences to inspire and engage. Need a new website? Running a campaign and want to engage audiences with some jaw dropping Motion Graphics? Luckily we have this and more in our bag of tricks.

View our services

Why we do it
DOING GREAT THINGS FOR GOOD PEOPLE

To satisfy our creativity and to keep true to our values Yoke strives to create captivating experiences for the right people. We love to work with those who are helping the world and trying their best to ensure our planet and its people are happy and healthy.

Learn more about us

TAKE ME TO THE TOP

Get in touch
Send us an email, give us a call or even be daring and come say hi in person.

By finger (easy)
Email: hello@thisisyoke.com
phone: 07971 679624
twitter: thisisyoke
skype: thisisyoke

By foot (a little more effort)
Yoke Design
133 Cumberland Road
Bristol
BS1 6UX

©2012 Yoke

yoke | Doing great things for good people.

yoke

Work
Services
About us
Contact us
Blog

IT'S NOT WHAT WE DO IT'S HOW WE DO IT

yoke

Work
Services
About us
Contact us
Blog

IT'S NOT WORK IT'S A WAY OF LIFE

Our Services

Websites
DESIGN, BUILD, STRATEGY

With the internet going mobile the delivery of your content and users behavior has changed. Websites now need to work on a multitude of devices and platforms, big and small. This represents a challenge for us and an opportunity for you to reach more of your community. Fortunately we like challenges.

Learn more

Branding
IDENTITY, LOGO, BRANDING

Having a strong identity is the foundation for your visual communication. Yoke will work closely with you to find out what embodies your business, before translating that onto paper and screen. It's much more than just a logo, we create guidelines for colour, photographic style, typography and tone of voice.

Learn more

CMS
E-COMMERCE, OPEN SOURCE, WORDPRESS

Having the power to manage the content of your site and update it when you want gives you valuable autonomy and gives us more time with our colouring pens. We can provide simple elegant WordPress solutions to fully fledged e-commerce sites to get your online shop selling.

Learn more

Motion Graphics
AFTER EFFECTS, HD, VIDEO

With the advent of smart Tv's and handheld devices and the advance in download speeds users are expecting a much richer online experience. Motion Graphics gives us the possibility to really make things move for you and your audiences.

Learn more

Flash
SENSING, HTML5, EXPERIENTIAL

Flash is the technology that allows us to push your ideas further by creating animated, immersive online experiences. Flash is a "can-do" technology and we use it when other platforms can't deliver, this is why we like it and continue to use it where its needed. It has been our companion for some time now and we know our stuff.

Learn more

3D
ILLUSTRATION, CHARACTER, SITE VECTORS

3D is another toy in our box that we like to bring out when we want to impress. We love using it for illustration, weaving it into motion graphics or adding 3D content to immersive site experiences. It is another one of those tools that allows us to go further for our clients and really make their ideas stand out.

Learn more

Our Process

We have a foundation process that applies to all of our work, be it an immersive 3d animation short, to a full e-commerce website. From these strong foundations the project will go from strength to strength as everyone involved will know exactly what to expect and by when.

Planning
STAGE 1 IN THE FOUNDATION

This stage starts off with a coffee and a sit down to discuss your goals and how best these can be achieved. At this point its all about building the framework that the project will sit in and grow. Budgets, timelines and important milestones will be sketched but more importantly we have the

The Latest and Greatest

Zero Waste Events
CMS, PROJECT, SUSTAINABILITY, WEBSITE

Campaign website to make the London 2012 Olympic Games Zero-Landfill.

Read more

Too Good To Waste
CMS, MOBILE, PROJECT, WEBSITE

Campaign website to reduce food waste in restaurants.

Read more

Organic Farming
CMS, BRANDING, FARMING & FOOD, PROJECT, WEBSITE

Making life easier for an Organic Farming Research and Education Centre.

Read more

AV Arts
BRANDING, PROJECT, WEBSITE

Create a common ground to bring together an artistic community.

Read more

Eco Trekking
BRANDING, PROJECT, TRAVEL, WEBSITE

Help establish an Eco tourism industry in Northern India.

Read more

Eco Earth Textiles
BRANDING, PROJECT, WEBSITE

Give a new lease of life to an ethical textile trader's online store.

Read more

Life before Yoke

"We are no spring chickens. yoke has been built from years of experience in the creative industry"

We have created work for some really big names, some of which you may have heard of before. This means that we have a wealth of expertise and knowledge to share. Take a look at our personal portfolios below to get a flavour of what we have done in our previous lives.

Alister Wynn
View portfolio

Jay Bigford
View portfolio

Before yoke we created things for...

 orange™ | TRIUMPH | PEUGEOT | OXFORD UNIVERSITY PRESS

 O₂ | NHS | NOKIA | SHARP

 WALKERS | WE ARE MACMILLAN. CANCER SUPPORT | KIA | DOLBY

 Disney | BBC | Green Party | Sun Life Financial

MTV | WRIGLEY

 View our services

www.sundancechannel.com/fullfrontalfashion

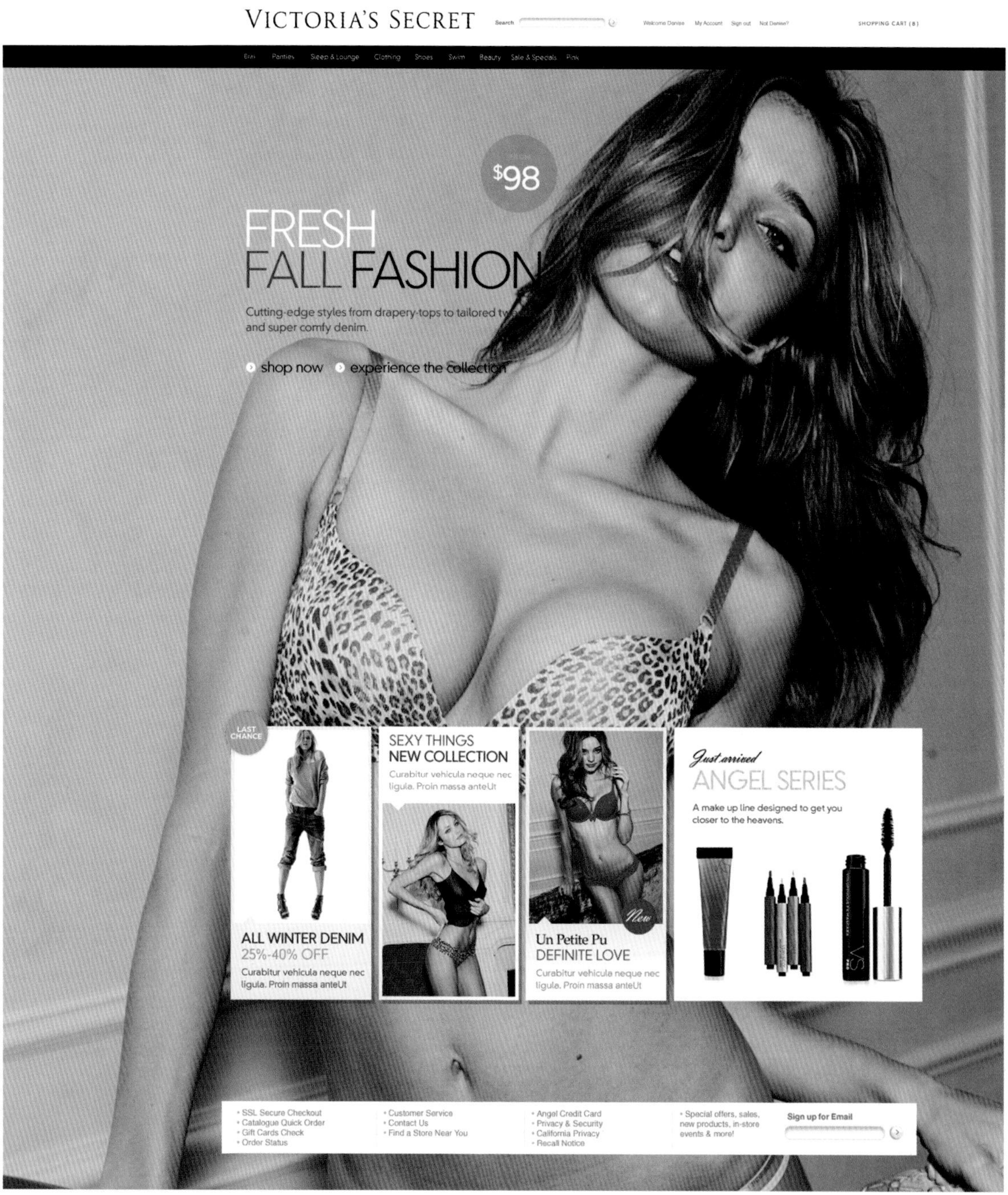

www.victoriassecret.com

DENIMMOVES

tigerofsweden.com/denimmoves

www.gilt.com